Arbitrage

The authoritative guide on how it works,
why it works, and how to make it work for you.

Chris Green

PBLLC Press, Rehoboth, MA

2012

Arbitrage

The authoritative guide on how it works, why it works, and how to make it work for you

Green, Christopher John

Hi, Mom!

Edited by Chiara Therisod & Tom Sutton

Published by PBLLC Press, Rehoboth, MA 02769

First Printing, September 2012

ISBN-13: 978-1478251897

ISBN-10: 1478251891

Printed in the United States of America

Cover design by Stebbings Partners, stebbings.com

Arbitrage

The authoritative guide on how it works,
why it works, and how to make it work for you.

Dedicated to my loving wife, Jenn.

Without her love and support, none of this would be possible.

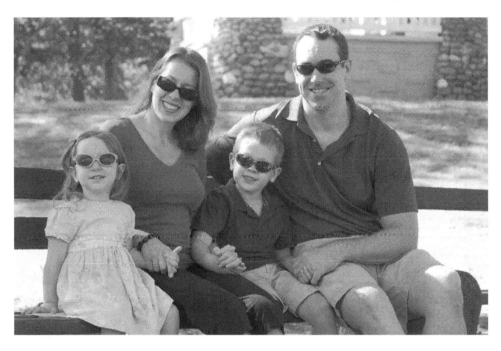

This book is the result of a lifetime of learning. I am very thankful for support that I've received from family and friends along the way. The last five years have been one amazing ride. Not everyone gets to work with amazing people and amazing products everyday and it is even more rewarding when those products are able to produce a positive change in so many people's lives.

Did you know that every month we give away ScanPower SWAG? Sunglasses, Carton Clips, even T-Shirts!

Just visit scanpower.com/winstuff and enter your email address for your chance to win.

Some of this stuff you can even buy on Amazon!

ScanPower shades: amazon.com/dp/B00JQHQ5QQ

Carton Clips: amazon.com/dp/B00C3V89XE

When Chris Green talks, FBA sellers listen.

Opportunity Summary

We live in an amazing time! Entrepreneurs now have access to powerful tools and information that were simply not possible just a few, short years ago. Barriers to entry have been shattered and small entrepreneurs can now compete with the big boys on the biggest stages practically from day one. Information has always been power, but never before in history has information been so powerful and at the same time nearly universally accessible. A smartphone in your pocket gives you access to Wikipedia, your Kindle library, a few thousand apps, GPS, and let's not forget this little thing called the Internet. The next wave of successful entrepreneurs wlll be the ones who use this information to their advantage. When you see the world this way, you see that there are so many opportunities all around you. Since time is limited, you can't do them all; so find your passion, find people who share your passion, and take action!

Setting up an Amazon business that utilizes the Fulfillment By Amazon (FBA) program is much like buying a franchise opportunity. With a franchise, you buy a package, get some knowledge and equipment to get started, and then it's up to you to run with it. One of the big differences is that buying and selling online using FBA really has no 'buy-in'. There are no major upfront costs to get started. All you really need is a little knowledge, some motivation, and some inexpensive tools and services. You probably already have a computer with an Internet connection at home in order to list products for sale and a smartphone like an iPhone or Android phone that you can use to gather pricing information on products.

It is common to underestimate the real, legitimate income that can be generated by this business because it is a business that truly does not have a high cost of entry.

Arbitrage: The authoritative guide on how it works, why it works, and how to make it work for you is the first book of its kind to provide a complete and exhaustive look at the fascinating world of arbitrage and resale.

This book is intended to be much more than just descriptive information about topics related to arbitrage and selling online. This book explains the WHY behind everything that you'll be reading. Sure, I could stop by just explaining what FBA is, but the important part is understanding WHY FBA works. I could tell you how to price FBA items, but I want you to understand WHY you can price them that way. I could tell you that you can buy retail products from local retailers to sell online for big profits, but I want you to understand WHY you are able to find the same product at dramatically different prices from two separate places and WHY some buyers are willing to pay much more for that same product from a different sales channel.

It's the difference between giving you a fish, and teaching you to fish.

In this book, you learn about the primary market (retailers, both brick & mortar and online) and the secondary market (Amazon third-party sellers and eBay). You'll also learn to understand SUPPLY and DEMAND and how they affect PRICE, as well as how TIME affects all three.

In this book, I will give you the keys to the Arbitrage Kingdom with the mindset of unlimited opportunities and abundance rather than one of scarcity. The techniques described in this book can be used by anyone, anywhere to build a small side business or large empire. The only limit is your imagination.

So, what is arbitrage?

In a nutshell, arbitrage is the practice of taking advantage of a price difference between two or more markets, striking a combination of matching deals that capitalize upon the imbalance. The difference between these two market prices is the profit realized by whoever brings the deal together.

Think of it this way; you want to be able to 'SEE' items that are selling locally or online for much less than what they are selling for elsewhere online (such as Amazon or eBay). These items represent the potential for arbitrage opportunities (and profit).

At the same time, you want to avoid items that cost more locally or online than what they sell for elsewhere online.

When you have the right information, it's like you have special goggles that allow you to see all of the opportunities around you (while those without the information simply cannot).

Remember this: the markets are terribly inefficient and buyers do not make all buying decisions based solely on price. Identical items sell for different amounts in different places all day, every day. Sometimes items are less expensive at local retailers; sometimes they are less expensive online. When you can identify these differences, you can be the one who profits by matching the lower cost supply with the higher priced demand.

Arbitrage is a word that was generally used in financial markets, but we have brought it over to the world of physical products. Sites like Amazon and eBay have given small sellers access to customers worldwide and services like Fulfillment By Amazon (FBA) have allowed these sellers to scale their businesses in ways never before possible. There is really no limit to what you can arbitrage!

Arbitrage is just the beginning.

This book is designed to be the first in a series of books that build upon each other. The business of arbitrage is simple in principle; buy low and sell high with the profit is the difference between cost and sale price.

Once you have mastered the principles of arbitrage and margin, it's just a matter of deciding what kind of business you want to pursue.

Are you trying to replace your current income and quit your job?

Are you trying to make a million dollars?

Are you just trying to make some extra money and retire a few years early?

There is no one-size-fits-all answer of which business model is best. Each seller will have their own goals and risk-tolerance levels.

Subsequent books in this series will explore sourcing strategies for both retail and online, as well as sourcing strategies specifically for used books and media items. Putting all of this information in one monster, all-inclusive book would be overkill. The book would be HUGE and even intimidating to a new seller. Not all of the information contained in the book would even apply to every reader. Consider this a modular approach to book writing; get the books that apply to your business goals, and leave the ones that don't.

I've written two other books that deal with in-depth strategies for retail and online sourcing called:

Retail Arbitrage: Sourcing Secrets for buying retail products to resell for BIG PROFITS

For more information and exclusive offers, please visit:

RetailArbitrage.com

Online Arbitrage: Sourcing Secrets for buying products online to resell for BIG PROFITS

For more information and exclusive offers, please visit:

OnlineArbitrage.com

A list of all available books can be found at: scanpower.com/books

Things change over time.

At the time of this writing, all links, fees, rules, and laws are represented accurately. It is always best to check the current web pages for any changes that may have occurred between the writing of this book and when you start your business. The fees to sell on Amazon.com and eBay.com can change and will affect prices and payouts. Laws may change regarding paying and collecting sales tax.

I suggest finding a good certified public accountant (CPA) that can help steer you in the right direction. Like any service, they should save you more money than they cost you. If they don't, fire them!

Earnings Disclaimer

I can't make any promises as to how much money you'll make in this business. It's up to you to go out and run with this information. I can't promise that you will make a certain amount of money, or any money, or not lose money, as a result of following the information in this book. What I can do is give you as much useful and accurate information that I can and trust you to learn it and use it to the best of your ability.

I'll show you deals that we have done and the profits that we made but there is no guarantee that you will be able to replicate them exactly. With any business, your results will vary and will be based on your personal abilities, knowledge, and level of desire (among other things). Each person's results will vary.

The use of the information provided in this book should be applied and used based on your own due diligence and you agree that we are not liable for your success or failure.

Basically, we can help, but it's up to you to actually run your business. ☺

The good news is that we are here and we are happy to help!

To your success,

-Chris Green

Director, ScanPower

Want to connect? Message me @ facebook.com/chris

ScanPower is the leader in Amazon and FBA news and content. We offer so much incredible content and information that it can be difficult to keep up. Here are the best ways to connect:

SpreeCast – Weekly LIVE video/radio shows about Amazon, FBA, and more! Special guests include online sales tax experts from TaxJar.com and deal experts from FatWallet.com.

spreecast.com/users/chrisgreen

ScanPower Monthly Magazine – Monthly publication available on Amazon in PRINT and KINDLE formats. Highlights the news around Amazon, FBA, online selling, and ScanPower.

scanpower.com/magazine

Are you on Facebook? The **ScanPower Facebook Group** is widely considered the best place to get Amazon and FBA information as well as get any questions answered by experienced online sellers. If you have a question about getting started, ask it here and get up and running.

facebook.com/groups/scanpower

YouTube – The ScanPower YouTube channel has replays of past SpreeCasts as well as demonstration videos of sourcing tips and tricks.

youtube.com/scanpowerTV

SoundCloud – Podcast audio replays of the ScanPower SpreeCasts are available for download or streaming from SoundCloud.

soundcloud.com/scanpower

ScanPower LINK – This is a dedicated app that pulls in the posts from the Facebook group, the latest YouTube videos, SoundCloud files, SpreeCasts, and ScanPower Events, all on one place.

Android: bit.ly/SPLinkAndroid

iPhone: bit.ly/SPLinkiPhone

ScanPower University

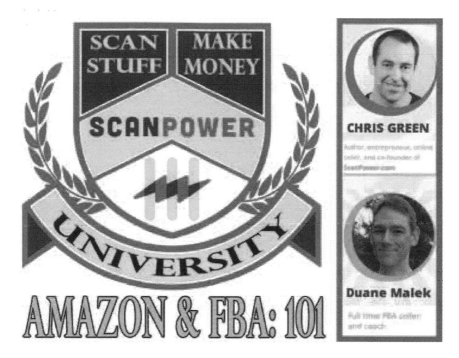

ScanPower University is the one-stop FAST TRACK to getting started with Amazon and FBA (Fulfillment By Amazon)! Lead by Chris Green, Director of ScanPower and Duane Malek, full-time FBA seller and coach.

This course is designed to take a new Amazon seller from having little to no knowledge of Amazon and FBA to a full understanding of how it works, why it works, and completely finish their first FBA shipment.

ScanPower University includes membership in a PRIVATE Facebook Group only for ScanPower University members. This means you have a dedicated place to get the answers you need about getting started with Amazon and FBA! Members also get access to monthly PRIVATE SpreeCasts with Chris and Duane as they host an ASK-ME-ANYTHING SpreeCast! This SpreeCast is PRIVATE and only for members of

ScanPower University (including lifetime access to all of the past and future episodes). The ScanPower University course outline includes step-by-step video modules to walk you through every step of learning the business of successfully selling on Amazon and using FBA including:

- Understanding Amazon rules and policies

- Taxes, business license, CPAs, and more

- Introduction to product sourcing

- Creating your first FBA shipment

Plus ongoing support to ensure your success on Amazon!

scanpower.com/university

For the latest updates, new releases, and additional features, always check the website:

http://scanpower.com

Arbitrage: The Authoritative Guide

Table of Contents

Introduction

So, who is this Chris Green guy and how does he know so much about arbitrage? How did ScanPower get started? I'm glad you asked! Here's the whole story.

I've been selling online since 1999 and since then I've personally sold over two million dollars worth or merchandise.

This all started back when I was in the sixth grade, at a time when I had never heard of a thing called arbitrage. Like many kids my age, I was too busy collecting sports cards. Growing up in Canada, hockey cards were the most popular. I became fascinated that one card could be worth so much more than another. I didn't care who was on the card; I was more interested in the values and how they changed. I would read the price guides every month and track 'values' as they went up and down. I had a paper route that put about $25/week in my pocket and I would buy and sell sports cards at the local weekly card show. It got to the point where I would browse the card show and identify cards that one dealer was selling for a price that was too low, and flipping them to another dealer who was pricing them too high. I would find one dealer would place a value on a card that was too low, and I'd find another dealer who placed a higher value on that same card and I'd have a buyer lined up before I even paid for the card. Little did I realize where all this was heading.

Fast-forward a few years when my family moved to Texas when I was 13 years old. My aunt was a jewelry dealer who would have high-end jewelry shows in her home. One summer I was at a garage sale and found a pile of gold necklaces with a gold flower and pearl pendant on them. They appeared to be new and were all individually bagged. The seller had a price of $1.50 a piece on them. They weren't real gold or anything but they looked nice and I was hoping that my aunt could put them in her jewelry shows, even if just as an inexpensive option for her clients. I bought all twenty of them and brought them over to see what she thought. She said that I did well! She said she could easily sell these in her show. She bought them all from me for $10 each. Sweet! Easy money, right? Of course I was still young and naïve, and briefly felt bad, even cheated, when I found out that she sold them in her show for $25 each. For a moment I thought that I should be the one getting $25 but then I started to realize that she did work as well with organizing the show and that she took a risk as well buying them from me. I was acting as a middleman and so was she. Why did I sell for $10? Because I was happy with the price! Just because I found out later that she sold them for more should not change that fact.

This one was a two-step process to get the supply and demand to meet. There was a demand for this item at $25 that would have never found the products at $1.50, but between my aunt and myself, we were able to match supply with demand and both realize a profit along the way.

She also instilled in me the concept of 'value'. Just because someone says it is 'worth' something, doesn't mean that it will sell for that price. I would get caught up with this from the sports cards days where a price guide would say a card is 'worth' a certain value. She would tell me it's only worth something if someone is willing to pay it. On Amazon, this is known as the difference between what an item is 'listed for' and what it is 'selling for'.

Now let's fast forward to my college years. It's now 1996 and this fancy new thing called the Internet is quickly becoming popular. This was the dawn of a new day in terms of matching sellers with buyers. EBay was a magical site where anyone could sell anything to anyone in the world! You could also search for and find anything that you may have been looking for at garage sales for years. Being a child of the 80's, I was into Transformers. With the Internet, so much more information was now available. I learned that when the US television show stopped airing, it continued on in Japan. There was a whole new series of Transformers cartoons that had never been seen or even heard of by most US Transformers fans. This was too cool; I wanted these videos! I originally wanted them just for myself but it quickly became apparent that there were lots of people like me who would pay for these videos. Out of all of these potential buyers, some would pay a little, but some would pay a lot. Knowledge is power and I had the knowledge of where to get them so I bought and sold cartoon videos to pay my way through college. My roommates all thought it was pretty crazy, but it paid the bills. This market unfortunately dried up for two reasons. First, even though I was the first to enter this specific market, when there is money to be made, other sellers will eventually find it, enter the market, and prices will fall. They will fall until the equilibrium price is met. Second, the number of people who grew up in the 80's and still wanted to watch Transformers cartoons is fairly small and once the people in this market have purchased them, the market is pretty much dead. It is not an ongoing, sustainable market in the same sense like the Star Wars brand, which stands the test of time with old fans and new ones alike all across the world.

As fate would have it, I ended up getting a degree in Economics.

So, I finally graduated and found a job in sales with Bosch Power Tools calling on Home Depot and Lowe's (known as the home center channel). I did this for five years and it is what propelled me into a full time arbitrage-business owner. You see, when you are in a Home Depot almost every day for five years, you notice things; things like product cycles where new models replace old models. The old models get clearanced out, sometimes at ridiculous prices. You see seasonal cycles as well as lucrative promotions such as Buy-One-Get-One-Free on top of an already-discounted clearance price.

Here was this enormous pool of inventory that could now be purchased for prices well below the market price. When you pair this with the Internet opportunities on eBay and Amazon, you've just struck a golden balance where you can be as big as you want to be with practically no risk. It means that you can buy your inventory on credit card and just wait for a buyer. And if you can't find a buyer, you can get a full refund! (I don't recommend making a habit of buying, holding, and returning, but this is a safety net that can be used as a new seller 'tests the arbitrage waters'. There is more information about the zero-risk way to start at the end of this book in Bonus #4).

Purchasing inventory at the retail level meant that you had none of the restrictions of buying from manufacturers. There were no minimum order quantities and no pricing agreements. You buy your inventory and you can do whatever you want with it.

All the pieces were in place to take this thing to the next level. There was demand out there that valued these items at prices higher than what I could get them for. But without the Internet and sites such as eBay and Amazon, that demand would not be able to find that supply. And if I didn't buy the supply and make it available to that demand, then this supply and demand would never meet. Without each piece, the sources, the prices, and the ability to get the supply to the demand through the Internet, this business wouldn't work.

On top of all these pieces falling into place, I was working in Dallas, Texas where there were over sixty Home Depots within a one-hour drive. Let's run some numbers (simplified example): a $300 item goes clearance for $100. I can sell for $200 and make $100 profit. Buyer is getting a $300 item for $200 and is happy with the deal. I find the twenty Home Depots that have the highest inventory levels and go out and pick up an average of ten units from twenty stores. In one day, I am able to get 200 units at $100 profit a piece. $20,000 profit on just one item, one day of the year. I think you can now see where this is going.

Arbitrage on a grand level was starting to take place.

I was still limited by my regular full-time job, even though it was great to keep me in the stores to spot the latest trends and price changes. It got to a point where I had to make a choice and the choice was to quit and go full time in arbitrage and selling online. Thankfully we had over 2,000 square feet of storage space to store products and pack and ship orders (this was still the pre-FBA days). It was getting big, it was generating great income, but I was running into the same limitations that plague all online sellers: Space and time restrictions. We can only store so many products in a limited amount of space and we can only manage so much of the business (including packing and shipping orders) with a limited amount of time in each day. My wife was helping a great deal at this time and the business was slowly taking over our lives. If we ever wanted to go out of town to visit family, the whole thing had to be shut down.

Enter Fulfillment By Amazon, or FBA.

This is the piece of the puzzle that takes arbitrage to a whole new level. What FBA is and why it works so well will be explained in greater detail in Chapters 3 & 4, but the basics of FBA are that Amazon will store, sell, pick, pack, and ship your items for you. FBA does all this at a price that allows you to maintain profitable margins. Even the storage fees are so low that it doesn't make sense to store your own products. With one new service, we could now remove both the space and time restrictions that were limiting the growth of our online business.

The additional piece that makes FBA work is understanding the Amazon customer. When a seller uses FBA, all of their items are eligible for the same free shipping programs as Amazon's own inventory such as Free Super Saver Shipping and Amazon Prime. The reason that we were so quick to adopt the FBA program is that we BOUGHT so much from Amazon. We were pretty much Amazon power-buyers and had been Amazon Prime members since the day Prime was announced. We valued the fast shipping and customer service that you get with every Amazon order. We knew that there were tons of other buyers out there just like us who would choose our products over our competitor's products, even at a higher price because they were FBA items (much more on this later in the book).

So we sent everything to FBA warehouses and we are still 100% FBA today. Processing orders and packing boxes is not hard, but we would rather spend our time on the most profitable parts of our business and sourcing new products.

This is when we first got into books and media items.

I was browsing online one day and came across the barcode scanners that people were using to tell them the online value of books. This was fascinating. You could scan a barcode and see what the market price was for a book, then compare it to your cost, calculate profit, and make buying decisions. Too cool; I was hooked and I was in. I was buying books and listing them as fast I could. It was great that I had a new product line, but now I was back to shipping my own orders again. At first, I thought that there was no way that FBA could be used on books. After all, books were used, onesie-twosie type items and not new, multiple quantity, commodity-type items like the power tools we were used to sending in. When Amazon said that the FBA program could be applied to used books, a whole new world opened up before me. Right away, all books and media were labeled and sent to FBA.

Now we had a new problem. Time and space restrictions were gone, but now the business had a new bottleneck – speed. We could get products to sell online; that was not hard. And we could sell them with FBA, which was also not hard. The new bottleneck was getting the items prepared for FBA. We couldn't get the items listed fast enough, priced properly (FBA items are priced much differently, more on this later), and labeled in an efficient manner. We were touching every item multiple times so the workflow was not optimal. The final straw was when my wife and I had over 400 books and media items facing spine up on the kitchen table. We each had sheets of FBA labels in our hands and we were scanning items over and over again trying to match up these items with the labels. It took us forever and we only hoped that we didn't make any mistakes.

We needed a new system, so I posted a short job description on the freelance developer website, elance.com. This is where I met Paul Retherford who is currently the CTO of ScanPower. When Paul and I first talked, FBA was still a very new and widely unheard of service. What I was describing in my job description was something that had never been done before. We talked back and forth many times before the job was approved and work started. I still remember the first item that I processed through version 1.0 of this software (it wasn't even called ScanPower at this point). The FBA label printed out individually and instantly as I processed the book. This was powerful stuff. A whole new world of online selling was about to begin. Paul and I talked about making the software available to other FBA sellers. After many discussions, we named it ScanPower and we agreed to be partners. We actually worked on ScanPower for over a year before ever actually meeting in person. ScanPower was released in July 2010 and the rest is history!

This new arbitrage business model was about to take off.

Almost all of the pieces were in place to create a powerful, 100% scalable, nearly risk-free business model that literally anyone can do with no prior experience. FBA was there to do all of the storing, selling, picking, packing, shipping, and customer service. ScanPower was there to help sellers process inventory fast and price their FBA items properly. There was still one piece that did not exist.

You see, the scanning tools available were all designed for books and media only and designed for sellers who processed their own orders. This made sense when it was only booksellers who bought and sold only books and shipped all of their own orders (pre FBA days). When you use FBA, you quickly realize that you can buy and sell practically anything! This changed the needs of the scanning programs.

We needed a scouting program that could scan any barcode on any product and provide pricing data for every item on Amazon, not just books. The scouting programs that were available were simply not good enough, so we had to make our own. It was built from the ground up and designed specifically for arbitrage through FBA. We called it ScanPower as well. It was first available on Android devices and is now available for iPhone and iPad as well. There is nothing like it in terms of power in your hand to make the best buying decisions at the lowest risk. Profitable items are everywhere! Retail stores, pharmacies, grocery stores, you name it. Book sales are fun and thrift stores are great, but they can be some of the most competitive environments. And some book sales are only once or twice a year, while some retail stores are open 24 hours a day. ScanPower was the last piece of the puzzle that would allow anyone, anywhere, to identify any opportunity around them. Put it all together with ScanPower to get your items to FBA fast and efficiently and you're now leveraging FBA to sell your products to more customers at higher prices. You now have a truly remarkable business model that simply did not exist in this form just a few short years ago. It is an exciting time to be selling online and it will only get bigger and better. Amazon is growing at a remarkable rate and at the same time providing their third party sellers with powerful tools to compete with big, established companies from day one.

Sellers who see the opportunities in front of them and take action will be building an amazing business for themselves; a business that many sellers would describe as too good to be true. As you read through this book, test what I've written and see if it isn't 100% accurate.

You may be thinking that as a seller myself, wouldn't I be inviting competition by not only letting other sellers use the ScanPower software, but also by writing a book and teaching others how arbitrage works and all the secrets about how to do it? The truth is that I'm not. I know that I am a small fish in the vast ocean that is online selling. There are so many different products that it would be irrational for me to think that I could somehow go out and get ALL of the deals (more on this in Bonus #3 at the end of this book).

Think of it this way; there are over 2,000 Home Depots in the United States. Calculate it out with travel time and it would take an entire year to go to each store once (and of course be away from home all year long). And don't think that Home Depot only has one deal a year; if I only went once a year, I would miss out on all the other deals throughout the year. This says nothing about Target, Wal-Mart, Toys R Us and Big Lots deals that are out there every day.

As for teaching people, we are in a unique position in this industry. We are not just a group of programmers who decided to make something that we think sellers might need. ScanPower has features that I know sellers need because I am a seller. They were designed by me and for me; we just let other people use them because we are super nice guys. I know what pricing information I need in order to make a good buying decision and that's why it is included in ScanPower. I enjoy helping other sellers use our products optimally. Hearing success stories from our users makes it a very rewarding business to be a part of. ScanPower is pretty much the industry standard when it comes to FBA and when sellers know how to use FBA optimally, the utility of our programs becomes very evident. Still, no one has to use our programs. There is a whole bonus chapter later in the book (Bonus #4) explaining how to start an arbitrage business with zero risk and not use any of our programs.

Well, that's my story. That's where I started and this is where I am today. Arbitrage is just something that I've always been good at, I suppose. I feel very blessed to be part of a team where we all do what we are individually good at and we are able to create something powerful and useful that other people can use to their own success.

There is a lot of information out there and there are a lot of experts popping up. Some are great, some are good, and some simply do not know what they are talking about. As with any business, test the methods and test the author.

Personal guarantee:

I've tried to write this book as accurately and concisely as possible. Sometimes it can be difficult to write out details that are better explained in a one-on-one conversation. This is an entirely new type of business and the exact concepts of WHY it works are not always easy to grasp the first time around.

If you have any questions about this business, I invite you to call or email me directly.

214-298-6866 – yes, that is my cell phone number and I invite you to call (or send a text message if that's your thing). I'm Eastern Standard Time so please consider the time when calling. Also, please read the whole book before you call. ☺

If you prefer email: chris@scanpower.com

For general technical support for ScanPower, please visit the support & help pages at http://www.scanpower.com

Or send an email to support@scanpower.com and someone from the ScanPower support team will be happy to help.

Conflict of Interest?

There will be some people who read this book and believe it to be nothing more than a book to get people to sign up for our programs. I assure you that it is not. I'll write it right here: you do not need to use any of our programs to run a successful arbitrage business.

If I wrote a book that was simply designed to get a ton of people to sign up for ScanPower but didn't explain the ins and outs of the arbitrage business, then most would quit pretty much right away. Getting customers to sign up for ScanPower and then failing at this business and leaving after one month does not make any sense. The only way a seller stays with our programs is if they are successful! Do we want them to stay? Of course! So we want to do everything that we can to help them achieve that success. When they are successful, we are successful!

I promote FBA education. When sellers understand how to use FBA properly and optimally, they will see why we do the things that we do.

They will also see where our competitors fall short. Sometimes they simply just don't know what they don't know!

We are in a unique position in this industry. It is rare for a company to not only produce the best programs related to that industry, but to also have the best understanding of the industry and actively promote the education of that industry. There are other companies out there that will teach you to use their programs, but you are on your own to really understand and run your business. Do any of them possess such an in-depth understanding of the actual industry? And if so, are they willing to share so openly?

There may even be critics or detractors who claim that by sharing this information, it will 'destroy the market' or 'kill their business'. **This should be seen as a good sign as it means that they KNOW there is money to be made and they want to be the ones making it, not you.**

I believe that the free market will work itself out and that sellers who can compete will thrive in the good times and survive in the bad times. Those who cannot compete will go out of business.

I encourage all readers to read this book and evaluate what it says. Test what is written and decide for yourself if it is or is not accurate.

Chapter 1 – What is Arbitrage?

I'll be using the term arbitrage a lot in this book, so it's important that we give it a definition and understand what it means.

Let's start with the Wikipedia definition of Arbitrage:

http://en.wikipedia.org/wiki/Arbitrage

> In economics and finance, arbitrage is the practice of taking advantage of a price difference between two or more markets: striking a combination of matching deals that capitalize upon the imbalance, the profit being the difference between the market prices. When used by academics, an arbitrage is a transaction that involves no negative cash flow at any probabilistic or temporal state and a positive cash flow in at least one state; in simple terms, it is the possibility of a risk-free profit at zero cost.

> In principle and in academic use, an arbitrage is risk-free; in common use, as in statistical arbitrage, it may refer to expected profit, though losses may occur, and in practice, there are always risks in arbitrage, some minor (such as fluctuation of prices decreasing profit margins), some major (such as devaluation of a currency or derivative). In academic use, an arbitrage involves taking advantage of differences in price of a single asset or identical cash-flows; in common use, it is also used to refer to differences between similar assets (relative value or convergence trades), as in merger arbitrage.

> People who engage in arbitrage are called arbitrageurs—such as a bank or brokerage firm. The term is mainly applied to trading in financial instruments, such as bonds, stocks, derivatives, commodities and currencies.

Phew! That's a lot of fancy words to describe the many different forms of Arbitrage.

It is summarized here for simplicity:

Arbitrage is the practice of taking advantage of a price difference between two or more markets, striking a combination of matching deals that capitalize upon the imbalance. The difference between these two market prices is the profit realized by whoever brings the deal together.

This simply means that you find products that you can buy low and sell high. You're finding items to buy and sell for a profit. You're matching up supply and demand. You're identifying market inefficiencies and capitalizing (profiting) on your knowledge of these inefficiencies. **There are many different ways to say the same thing.**

A recurring theme of this book is that knowledge and information are POWER. Those who have the knowledge, those who have the information, have the power.

Without the knowledge and information, could you walk into a store and identify all of the items that have a higher value on the secondary market (Amazon or eBay) that can be purchased at a price that leaves room for profit for you? You can try to get some, but you'd never get them all. And you might bring some home that turn out to be complete duds. One of the most enjoyable parts of this business is when you find those items that you would never expect to have a high value online, yet they are items that you can find locally for so much less. Odds are, that without the proper information, if you didn't know it was a winner, neither did anyone else.

Arbitrage can also be called resale and those who buy products for resale are called resellers. These terms will also be used throughout this book.

Depending on the context, I'll also use the terms **Retail Arbitrage** and **Online Arbitrage**. These terms merely indicate the source of the products being resold.

Another important distinction to make when discussing arbitrage is the retail market and price compared to the secondary market and price. Retail stores are the primary market and they are bound by pricing agreements with manufacturers as to what prices they can or cannot charge. When supply and demand change rapidly, the price at retail stores is not affected. What is affected is the ability to purchase those products at the retail price. If demand spikes, then you may not be able to find any at retail stores, or the primary market, because all of the stores sell out.

On the secondary market, price is set by supply and demand exclusively. When demand for a product spikes and the supply available for sale stays the same, then the price on the secondary market goes up. This is all just simple economics and human behavior. When the price on the secondary market exceeds the price at retail stores, entrepreneurs, or resellers, will enter the market by purchasing any available product for the artificially low retail price and bringing that supply to the secondary market when the price set by high demand and low supply is much higher.

From the arbitrage definition: The PROFIT being the difference between the market prices.

When EBay first started, they brought an entirely new concept to the world of arbitrage. They basically allowed anyone, anywhere to sell anything to anyone. This created an open secondary market where price was set by supply and demand. It was so open that prices would often quickly return to the equilibrium price. It got to the point where it became difficult to find anything for a price lower than the eBay price. Sellers practicing arbitrage long before you could sell on Amazon were finding products to buy and selling them on eBay. If an item could be purchased for less than the market price on eBay, it ended up on eBay. EBay ended up being the baseline of low prices online.

While eBay still represents some opportunities for retail and online arbitrage, as well as some strategies for selling at higher margins when prices and market conditions on Amazon change, for the most part this book is about arbitrage using Amazon.com as your primary sales channel.

Chapter 2 – Amazon vs. eBay

I am frequently asked the question of what are the differences between Amazon and eBay. While they are both places that you can use to sell products online, the similarities pretty much end there.

Product Pages vs. Listings

The simplest way to explain the real differences are to contrast the two methods used to display products to the buyer. Many people are familiar with the eBay way of doing things. Every seller creates listing pages for each of their items. When a buyer searches for an item, say a specific item like a DW959 DeWalt drill, eBay will display all of the item pages that match the search terms DW959, DeWalt, and drill. Some items will be DeWalt drills, some will be drills from another brand, and some won't be drills at all. The buyer has to wade through the jumbled results to find the listing pages that are actually for DW959 DeWalt drills and then click through and compare several different listing pages on eBay to find one that they would like to buy. There may be 50 different sellers selling this drill, and all of their listings, or offers, are mixed together in the search results. Some will be auctions, some will be Buy It Now listings, and some buyers will have better feedback than others or more favorable return policies than others. It is up to the buyer to make sure that what they are looking for is accurately represented in the eBay listing. They may be expecting a DeWalt drill kit with two batteries but the eBay listing mentions that it only comes with one. It is the buyer's responsibility to read the entire listing before making a buying decision. Comparing all of these listings can be an arduous shopping experience for the buyer.

Compare to Amazon where the DW959 DeWalt drill kit has a single product page. This page is where all of the different sellers list their price and description. Sounds pretty simple from a buyer's perspective. There is one place with a consistent product page where the buyer knows what they are buying. Amazon as the marketplace maintains the product page and requires that all sellers who list on the product pages sell items that are exact matches to the details on the product page. This makes it very easy for the buyer to shop and it is one reason why so many buyers continue to go to Amazon as their first choice when purchasing items online.

While eBay has traditionally been just a list or products in categories or a list of search results, I have seen them take steps towards an Amazon-type of product page on eBay. Hey, if it works for Amazon, make it work for eBay!

You may be thinking that if all sellers are listed in one place, and all sellers are required to sell the exact same item, then wouldn't price be the only thing that matters? Wouldn't the lowest-priced seller get all of the sales? It's a valid question, but I can tell you from years of experience that there are many more things that go into a buyer's buying decision other than price. This book will explain why and show you how to differentiate yourself as a seller in order to protect your margins and to allow you to stop competing on price alone.

Ways That a Seller Can Differentiate Themselves on Amazon

Let's back up a bit. The Amazon marketplace has product pages and all sellers have to list on those pages. This means the customer gets to see all offers in one place. Some sellers see no other way to differentiate themselves other than price, so they lower price in a race to see who can make the least amount of money without going out of business (don't do this).

Price – Amazon sorts the seller offers by price. The lower your price, the more visible you are (in theory, not always in practice).

Feedback – Buyers check a seller's feedback prior to purchasing. If you have higher feedback than your competition, you can often command a high price by inspiring greater buyer confidence. A seller's feedback rating is displayed as both a percentage and as a total quantity of feedback received. Some buyers prefer to buy from sellers with less feedback because they feel as if they are helping out 'the little guy' instead of buying from a large mega-seller.

Product Description – Many sellers use bland, generic product descriptions that do not inspire any buyer confidence. A buyer will often choose an identical item from a seller with an accurate, professional product description. They do this because they have more confidence that the seller takes the time to describe their items in greater detail compared to a seller who used a generic description for all of their items. Buyers can see when sellers put more time and effort into the listing and will have more confidence that the item that they receive will accurately match the seller's description. They may feel as though they are taking a chance when buying from a seller with a generic description.

Return Policy/Customer Service – Some sellers offer a more generous return policy that gives the buyer more confidence in choosing them as a seller in the event that something goes wrong with the product or the order. Amazon recently implemented a new seller policy that states that a seller must offer a return policy that is at least as favorable as Amazon's return policy.

Keep in mind that none of these things are absolutes. Buyers buy from different sellers for many reasons and those reasons are not even always rational. All things being equal, a buyer may choose one seller over another because they have a lower feedback rating in order to 'help them out'. Some sellers have store names that some buyers find offensive so they choose not to buy from them even at a lower price. Some buyers will favor a store name that they connect with and pay a higher price. Some sellers may have a witty description that makes the buyer laugh and the buyer buys from them. These things happen all the time.

FBA – This is the game changer and the most powerful way to differentiate yourself as a seller on Amazon. When you are an FBA seller, you are now able to offer things that your competition simply cannot offer. Your items are now part of Amazon's fulfillment network meaning that your items are now eligible for the same shipping options and promotions as Amazon's own items. Amazon spent how many millions building the most advanced shipping and distribution systems in history? Now your items can take advantage of this system! This is ridiculously powerful.

Using FBA to differentiate yourself means that you are able to cater to a powerful sub-group of all Amazon customers who put a high value on Amazons' fulfillment process. You may not get the next sale, or every sale, but you'll still get sales. The good news is that your sale is at a price that protects your margins. Amazon even lets buyers sort the offers page by only items that are eligible for Amazon Prime and Free Super Saver Shipping. This makes other sellers, regardless of price, simply disappear from the buyer's view.

Listing on Each Site

The listing process is very different between Amazon and eBay. Because Amazon has product pages already defined, all you have to do is tell Amazon that you have the item, how many you have, and what your price is. A few clicks and you are done.

EBay is more work because each product that you sell has its own product page that has to be created. That means typing out titles, taking and uploading pictures, writing descriptions, and setting all of your seller-specific settings on the eBay listing page.

What Items Sell Best on Each Site

Amazon and eBay are both great sites for selling stuff, but certain items certainly do better on each site.

Amazon is great for new items, commodity-type items, and items of which you have multiple, identical quantities. You can sell practically anything on Amazon (for a list of restricted items, refer to the Amazon rules in Chapter 12) and if it already has a product page, you can have your items offered for sale in a matter of seconds; just find the product page for the item, enter the quantity that you have for sale, enter your price, and you're done. If it's not on Amazon, you can choose to create a new product page. This is not difficult and normally requires a UPC on the product (UPCs can also be purchased, more information in Bonus #2 at the end of this book). It is more work than listing on an existing product page, but the good news is that you only have to create the product page one time. Creating new product pages can be very rewarding, as you can enjoy being the exclusive seller on Amazon.

EBay is great for items that may not have product pages on Amazon. EBay is also great for one-of-a-kind items as well as collectible items. Many collectors will always check eBay for those specific, hard-to-find items that may not get listed anywhere else.

Many items will sell well on both sites. An eBay buyer's money is not worth less than an Amazon buyer's money so don't turn away buyers or sales for no reason. Some buyers just go to eBay first out of preference or out of habit. They may still believe that Amazon only sells books.

Other Differences

Listing Fees

Amazon has no listing fees so you can list as many items as you like for free. This is a powerful position to be in. I like to use this fishing analogy: with no listing fees, it's like you are fishing (for sales). You can throw as big of a net (list items) as you want. You don't even have to catch much (get sales) each time you throw your net. With no listing fees, you can keep throwing your net over and over again. The sales that you get are all bonus.

Contrast this with eBay where you pay a fee for every item that you list, whether it sells or not. This prevents you from throwing a large net or even throwing a net at all. Listing fees, even if small, will restrict the size of the nets that sellers are able, or are willing, to throw.

Payment Processing

When it comes to payment processing, Amazon includes this in the commission that they charge in each category. This is important to remember when comparing the fee structures of selling on Amazon vs. selling on eBay. To process payments on eBay, buyers have to go through PayPal which has its own set of fees. When you compare Amazon commission to eBay fees + PayPal fees, you'll see the fees are pretty close.

One thing that still kills me about eBay is that they remain the only place on the planet where a buyer can buy something but not pay for it. When you sell on Amazon, there is no such thing as a non-paying bidder!

Better (easier) Buyers

It's nothing personal against eBay, but I place a huge value on simplicity. When you sell on Amazon, especially as an FBA seller, it will be pretty rare for you to get questions from buyers. On Amazon, the price listed is the price of the item. No auctions, no offers, no haggling. You won't get questions after the sale either, because Amazon will handle all of the customer service on FBA items (more on this in the next chapter).

Higher Prices

As a seller, you will generally enjoy selling items at higher prices on Amazon than on eBay. There are many reasons for this. If you have a background on eBay and you are coming over to Amazon, this is an important facet to consider. Amazon shoppers will generally know what they want and will want to find it, buy it, and get on with their lives. They are not interested in waiting for auctions to close or waiting on Best Offers to be responded to. They put a value on simplicity and this value translates into higher prices.

EBay is often seen as a garage sale while Amazon enjoys a position as more of a premium marketplace. This is nothing personal against eBay; this is just how many buyers and sellers generally view the two sites.

Feedback

On eBay, feedback is left much more often than it is on Amazon. You can expect to receive feedback on about 5-15% of all of your Amazon orders. Maintaining 100% positive feedback on eBay is doable and is a great source of pride for eBay sellers. On Amazon, it is nearly impossible to maintain 100% positive feedback. I would say that 98% positive on Amazon equates to 100% positive on eBay.

Amazon has a feedback scale of 1 through 5. I know some people who will say that they never give out a 5 out of 5 because that would mean that the seller would have no room for improvement. I do not agree with their reasoning, especially as a seller myself, but there are buyers out there like this. Some buyers will consider a 3 out of 5 to be positive feedback even though it is considered neutral feedback on Amazon. If you sell enough volume on Amazon, you will have this happen to your account. I warn you about this now so that when it inevitably happens to your Amazon seller account, you won't be surprised. Take it all in stride and remember that it is all just par for the course when you sell on Amazon.com. You'll get negatives that are undeserved and even feedback comments that the buyer meant to leave for another Amazon seller.

There are services out there that will help you get a higher percentage of your buyers to leave you feedback, but I don't really recommend them. One reason is that when you are an FBA seller, you have enough things going for you to differentiate yourself as a seller that having a greater quantity of positive feedback will not make a difference in the mind of a buyer. If you use a feedback requesting service, you also run the risk of receiving negative feedback that you would not have received if you had simply left your buyers alone. Some buyers simply do not want to leave feedback and don't want more email asking them to leave it. You may just be asking for a negative.

It is still important to keep your feedback as high as possible. It is more important to have a high feedback percentage than to have a high quantity of feedback. You should periodically check your feedback to see if you've received any neutral or negative feedback scores. If you get too many, you run the risk of having Amazon close your seller account. Amazon takes customer satisfaction very seriously (more on the rules of Amazon in Chapter 15). If you do get a negative feedback, contact the buyer through Amazon's messaging system and ask what you can do to correct the situation. Because buyer and seller interaction is not as common on Amazon as on eBay, there can easily be simple misunderstandings. If you are able to work with the customer to their satisfaction through communication and explanation, refund (partial or full), or some other form of customer service, you can then ask the customer if they would consider removing their negative feedback.

Do not ever make removal of negative feedback contingent upon your customer service. Take care of the customer first; work on removing the negative feedback later.

If you are not able to come to a resolution or if you are not able to reach the customer, then it can help to leave a follow up comment to any negative feedback comments that you may receive. Always stick to the facts and show that you care about customer service and stand behind your items. **Follow up comments on negative feedback are for your future customers, not to make any kind of statement to the buyer who left the negative feedback.** Potential buyers will look at your feedback and will notice how you deal with unsatisfied customers. Amazon buyers are smart and it they see that you extended great customer service to a buyer who left you negative feedback, they may choose to still buy from you. If you leave a snarky remark, it does not inspire any kind of confidence that you'll provide good customer service to your future buyers.

Later in this book you'll see why if you sell everything through FBA and sell all new items that it's actually pretty hard to get negative feedback (and what you can do in the event that you do).

Deciding What To Buy To Sell On Amazon

If you have been selling on eBay, then you probably already know that a great place to help you decide what to sell on eBay (and how to price it) is to view the Completed Listings. You can search for the item that you want to sell and you can see recently listed items that are either identical or similar. You can see if they sold, when they sold, and how much they sold for.

Advanced eBay sellers may be using a service called Terapeak. Terapeak offers additional Completed Listing data from eBay that is not available directly from eBay anymore. This is a subscription based service and the information that they provide can help you make better decisions about what to sell as well as help you decide how to price your eBay listings.

On Amazon, there are no sales histories. This is a policy from Amazon's legal department so don't expect this to change anytime soon. So if you can't see what has sold, when it sold, or for how much it sold, how do you make good decisions when deciding what to sell on Amazon as well as how to price your items?

Fair question, but let's back up a bit.

There are no guarantees when it comes to online sales. Just because an item sold last month for $300 on eBay and last week for $350 on eBay doesn't mean that it will sell this week for $300 or $350. Depending on the item, it may never sell again at any price. What you are deducing from eBay Completed Listings data and Terapeak information is the likelihood that an item will sell again, how quickly it will sell, and how much it will sell for. If an item has many completed listings on eBay and they are all fairly recent and all around the same price point, then it will be more likely that it will still sell in the near future at or near that same price. If an item only has one sale in the past two months as well as several Completed Listings on eBay with no winning bidder or buyer, then it will be <u>less likely</u> that the item will sell again quickly or at a price equal to the last successful eBay listing.

You are playing a guessing game on eBay. You are making educated choices by using all of the available data at your disposal, but you still have no guarantees.

It's the same way on Amazon. On Amazon, you have different data with which to make the same decisions as to which item to list for sale as well as what to set for your price. An Amazon listing will have a Sales Rank and competition. It may not seem like much, but you can extract a lot of information from what you see.

First, let's start with Sales Rank. Without going into extensive detail on Sales Rank, understand that Sales Rank is an indication of a recent sale and nothing more. If an item has sold recently, it will have a better Sales Rank than an item that has not sold recently at all. The item with the better Sales Rank will have a more recent sale or a higher quantity of recent sales than an item with a worse Sales Rank. When you can tell that the Sales Rank reflects a recent sale, then your next step is to decide how to price. Much more on what Sales Rank is as well as what it is not is covered later in Chapter 13.

The Amazon marketplace is an open marketplace. This means that everyone can see all of their competitor's prices. If an item has sold recently, you will not be able to tell exactly which seller made the sale or the exact price at which the last sale was made. What you can see is what all sellers are charging for the item. You'll find that on most items, sellers will be offering similar, competitive prices. There may be sellers that are offering the item at an abnormally high price. This is likely not what the last item sold for, but in rare circumstances such as only one FBA seller and an Amazon buyer needing the item quickly, it could be. You can make an educated guess at the market price by looking at the competition.

Amazon sellers can be very competitive; if there are multiple sellers for an item and absolutely no one is making any sales, then the Sales Rank will get worse and worse. You'll find that if this happens, some sellers will look to lower their price to attract sales. Many times other sellers will follow with price drops. As the price lowers and the item attracts buyers, Sales Rank will change.

Another easy factor to consider is the number of sellers for any specific item. This is especially true for FBA sellers who will have more at stake by listing and sending inventory to FBA instead of just listing it as merchant fulfilled. If there are multiple sellers selling the item for a certain price, then you know that each of these sellers consider this an item worth selling and worth selling for the price which they are charging. If lots of sellers deem an item good to sell on Amazon, then it is likely a good item for you to sell as well.

When it's all said and done, only you can decide if the item is good for you to sell because only you know your specific product cost, your risk tolerances, and your available funds for inventory.

There are no guarantees in online sales, so don't fall into analysis paralysis when deciding what to sell. Consider the margins on your items as well as your competition. Gather as much information as you can. There is a lot of information available on both eBay and Amazon; you just have to know where to look and how to read it.

Can eBay make a grand comeback?

Like I mentioned earlier, the majority of this book will be slanted towards selling on Amazon for simplicity and scalability. I believe that most new online sellers will be able to make more money with less effort on Amazon. As time goes by, this may change.

One thing to remember is that the principles of arbitrage are not exclusive to Amazon. EBay represents a lot of opportunities for the right products, and they have done an amazing job integrating listing tools into their mobile apps (iPhone, iPad, and Android devices).

Here is an excerpt from a blog post that I did in June of 2012 about getting back into eBay after hanging out with Jason Smith from Thrifting With The Boys (TWTB, http://www.thrifting-with-the-boys.com)

An Amazon Guy And An eBay Guy Walk Into A Bar…

Now I've done eBay before. I've packed 100+ boxes a day, day after day. I've been a Platinum Powerseller, but I left eBay a few years ago for the allure and simplicity of Amazon and FBA.

My primary eBay accounts can be seen here:

#1: www.locomodem.com

Sales: $1,453,843.86

Transactions: 25507

#2: recon_tools

Sales: $270,151.39

Transactions: 5528

Finding stuff to sell wasn't hard, but if I'm going to go back and give eBay another chance, I need to be able to somehow match the efficiency of Amazon with one-of-a-kind items that are best suited for eBay. After all, now I'm back to taking pictures, choosing categories, and writing descriptions. It was not that long ago that this meant getting out your camera, taking the pictures, uploading them to your computer, and then editing, resizing, and cropping as needed. This step alone would seem to be a deal breaker, but here's where technology has really stepped up in eBay favor.

With one of a kind items, there is really no way around taking pictures and entering item specifics; you just need a dead-simple way doing it.

So, with my renewed interest in eBay and my desire for efficiency, I end up talking to Cindy Johnston Sorley of www.bubbacandance.com. Cindy raved over eBay's new iPhone and iPad apps and about how fast she could list items, even one-of-a-kind items that required pictures and specific, detailed descriptions. Her enthusiasm was contagious, but I was admittedly skeptical. That night, I downloaded the eBay app to my iPad and gave it a whirl.

The solution is pretty elegant. There is an app for iPhone and iPod Touch (referred to as the Gold App) and a dedicated iPad app (referred to as the Blue App). Now you have the camera and computer all in one and you can list without even having a computer! I know some of you may be laughing at me for being late to this party, and that's OK, I can handle it.

The point that I would make to eBay is this: sellers like me left eBay for many reasons, one of which was not being efficient enough to scale properly (something that Amazon and FBA did wonderfully). Now eBay has apps that let sellers list one-of-a-kind items with efficiency and hardly anyone knows about it? eBay should be screaming from the rooftops about their new apps!

Here is a picture of their iPad app:

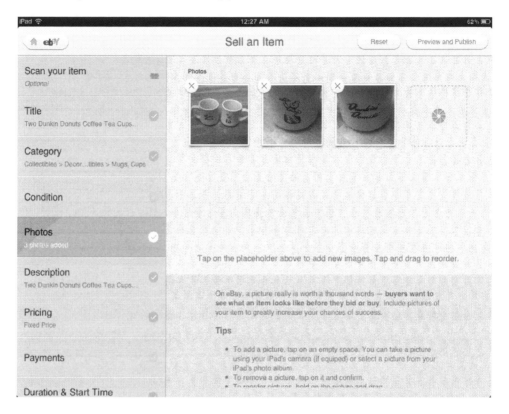

Did I mention that your phone makes a CHA-CHING sounds whenever you sell anything? Well played, eBay, well played.

I'll add another key piece of information about a huge strength that eBay has but, in my opinion, they do not promote well: they ability to be personal with your customers.

I attended eBay On Location (EOL) 2012 in Philadelphia, PA (this was my first eBay event).

I sold heavily on eBay for many years. While my recent focus has been on Amazon, now I'm taking a closer look at how eBay should be incorporated, not only into my online sales strategy, but how all sellers should appreciate some of the unique opportunities that eBay presents.

Some of this fresh look was inspired by the keynote presentation at EOL by Gary Vaynerchuk. I was fortunate to get to meet Gary after his presentation.

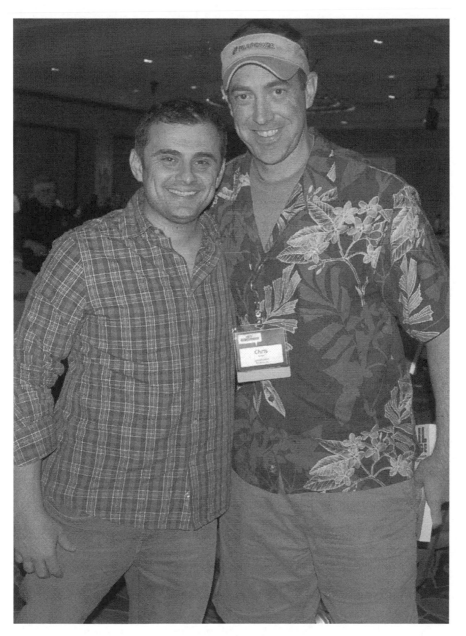

Gary wrote a book called *The Thank You Economy* (available on Amazon and be sure to watch the video) that lays out not only how easy it can be to be personal and engage with your customers, but also just how vital this practice is quickly becoming. Gary talked about how little things like hand written thank you notes in packages and following up with customers to personally thank them for their business are so easy to do, but so rarely done, that the companies that make the extra effort will be the ones earning their customers' business for years to come.

Is it just because customers are starting to expect an additional, personal level of service? Not entirely. It also has to do with the effect of social media and the newfound power of the customers' voice. An exceptional customer service experience can reach incredibly far through sites like Facebook or Twitter, and the same thing can be said for negative experiences.

In my opinion, one reason that many companies don't fully adapt a social media strategy is that it can be difficult, if not impossible, to accurately gauge the return on investment (ROI) of their efforts. If a company is too big, it can be difficult to get budgets and time approved for a social media strategy that's effective, and effective is, of course, a relative term when the exact ROI for the social media is often unknown. When it comes down to budget and time allocation, if you can't measure it, they probably aren't doing it.

The light bulb went off! While I was so busy thinking of all the ways that you could make money on Amazon, I lost sight of the big picture. Sure, I still believe that Amazon is easily the easiest place to sell online and make some real money both quickly and easily with the ability to scale, but at the end of the day, every customer that buys your products is **just another Amazon customer**. Amazon is happy with this arrangement, and many sellers are, too, as they watch the deposits in their bank accounts, but where is the long-term plan?

Like I mentioned above, when you sell on Amazon, that customer belongs to Amazon. Whether you ship yourself or use FBA, you are not allowed to market to that customer by email, phone, or even direct mail. This means no company link in your email signature, no packing slip in your outbound shipments, and nothing related to you personally can be packaged with your FBA inventory. If Amazon finds out that you are doing this, your selling privileges will be in jeopardy.

So what was I talking about? Considering eBay's place in your overall online selling strategy! The way I see it, eBay is one of the best places where you can gain exposure, engage with your customers, and use social media to provide that personal touch. Will each and every customer engage back with you? Unlikely, but social media is making this type of engagement easy to do and the companies that engage properly will be building a brand equity over time that will be difficult to catch without some long term planning by their competitors.

This is currently one of the BIGGEST differences between Amazon and eBay. With Amazon, you are getting sales, but when you run out of stuff to sell, no one will notice that you are gone. With eBay, you can build a brand and engage with your customers along the way. You can find out what they are interested in and you can find some common ground. Sellers should be using eBay strategically to gain incremental sales and take advantage of every opportunity to do things that your competition isn't doing. Engage with your customers in meaningful ways but don't summarize this information as an invitation to clobber your customers with marketing. They can even send them links to their Amazon store. Gary V calls this the jab, jab, jab, jab, jab, right hook.

This isn't something that can be built overnight and it isn't something that can be built disingenuously. My advice is to start now and BUILD your business in meaningful ways that your competition is likely overlooking.

What else did we do in Philly? Well, we took an eight-foot eBay sign to the Hard Rock Café, The Liberty Bell, and Independence Hall!

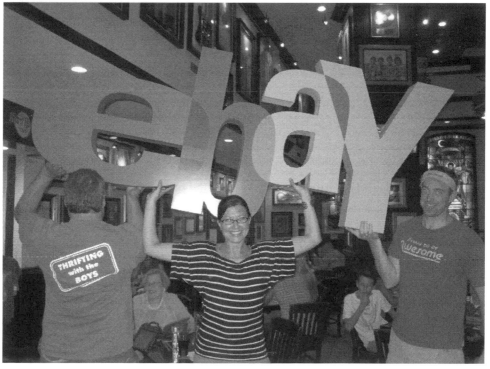

Chapter 3 – What is FBA?

Can you explain FBA in a few simple sentences? It's pretty much not possible (believe me, I've tried). FBA is simple in and of itself, but truly explaining what it is, why it works the way that it does, and how to leverage its power could take hours to explain and weeks to grasp. I've been almost 100% FBA for years and I've talked to hundreds of different FBA sellers and I'm still learning new things all the time. With that said, I'll do my best to explain everything that I know about FBA without too much rambling.

If you sell online, then you have likely already heard of Amazon's fulfillment program called Fulfillment By Amazon, or FBA. Sellers have been leveraging the FBA program for several years and the sellers who have embraced this new service and taken advantage of its capabilities have truly transformed their businesses.

Here is an incredible video of the inside of an Amazon FBA warehouse:

http://g-ecx.images-amazon.com/images/G/01/fba-tour/FBA-FC-Tour._V216203492_.html

FBA stands for Fulfillment By Amazon and it is Amazon's version of a fulfillment company. Fulfillment companies have been around for a long time and they are still around today, but there has never been anything like FBA before.

Traditionally, a fulfillment company would be a large warehouse that would store shippable products for many companies. When a company received an order for a product, that company would send the order to the fulfillment company who would then ship the company's product to the customer. The fulfillment company would charge the company for this service, while leveraging their large shipping volume to get good shipping rates. The fulfillment company does what they are good at which is storing inventory, picking, packing, and shipping orders while each company that uses the fulfillment company continues to do what they are good at which is selling their products. The companies also benefit by not having to have their own warehouse and shipping department to process all of their own orders themselves. It was a win-win relationship.

The difference between a traditional fulfillment center and Amazon's FBA program is that Amazon is not just the fulfillment company, they are also the marketplace. They have an active interest in seeing the products sell. Amazon makes money by charging a commission on the products sold on Amazon.com as well as the fees that they charge to use FBA (fees explained a little later).

So you are not just sending your products to a traditional fulfillment center and then left on your own to find customers and make sales. Amazon.com is the website that you are selling on and they are the ones doing the fulfillment for you. They WANT your items to sell just as much as you do; maybe even more so since they get paid whether you are making a profit or not. More on this later to make sure that you are maintaining margins and staying profitable. Additionally, FBA items are eligible for Amazon's shipping promotions including Free Super Saver Shipping and Amazon Prime. This is what makes FBA incredibly powerful. The FBA seller enjoys many advantages over their non-FBA competitors that will be explained in detail in the next chapter.

FBA can be described as a Triple Win.

Win #1. Higher prices, higher margins, higher payouts

Since items sold through FBA are eligible for Free Super Saver Shipping and Amazon Prime, FBA sellers actually raise their prices to match their competitor's total price (price + shipping). So even with the addition of FBA fees, the FBA seller still receives a higher net payout from their Amazon sale because of the higher sales price. For example, a seller who ships their own orders and sells an item for $20 with $5 shipping will show the same as an FBA seller selling the exact same item priced at $25.

Actually, the FBA seller will show first because FBA is the tiebreaker. That additional $5 that the FBA seller charges more than covers the additional FBA fees that they pay. Amazon is basically absorbing the shipping costs for you.

Win #2. Less work

FBA sellers sell items 24 hours a day, 7 days a week. Items ship all hours of the day or night including weekends. They ship whether the seller is at home or on vacation. Once an FBA seller prepares their items for the FBA warehouse and sends them to Amazon, they don't have to do anything else. They can monitor inventory levels and adjust prices as needed from anywhere with an Internet connection. They don't have to stock boxes, envelopes, packing materials, or shipping labels anymore. They also don't wait around for their UPS driver or go to the post office every day. You are outsourcing your entire shipping department.

Win #3. Happier Customers

It is estimated that 50% of Amazon buyers have never bought from a third party merchant. Amazon customers want to buy from FBA sellers. They trust Amazon and they know that their items will ship quickly and if there is ever a problem, Amazon will help (including an extended return policy). When your items are shipped through FBA (either for Amazon orders or Multi-Channel Fulfillment orders) they will attract these types of Amazon buyers who are willing to pay more to get their items shipped by Amazon. This is an important point to grasp: Amazon customers are willing to pay more for the exact same item if it comes from Amazon or an FBA seller. They do this because they know they will get their item fast and that customer service will be top notch.

Through FBA and third party sellers, Amazon has been able to expand the depth of the catalog of items that they can offer to their best customers.

Scalability Helps Small Sellers

The competitive advantages that the big sellers have enjoyed for years have vanished overnight with the introduction of FBA. A new seller on Amazon may have made some good money by selling items out of their garage in their spare time, but if they wanted to make a real income they would have had to scale up and get more space to handle more inventory and hire employees to help with all of the orders. Now they may make more money but they have additional overhead. There are two things that have kept small sellers small and those are space and time limitations.

As a small seller, you only have so much space in which to store products and you only have so much time to list, sell, and ship your orders. Ten orders a day can be fun. Twenty may get you excited. But can you fulfill 300 orders in a day? Can you do this day after day? And shut down your entire business if you ever wanted to go on vacation?

With FBA, you can grow your business as much as you want. FBA removes the space and time limitations and allows you to compete on the same playing field as the big, established sellers on day one. There are no scalability restrictions with FBA. If you have access to products, you could sign up with FBA and ship them fifty thousand products in one day and be selling 500 items a day within the week. Manage your inventory properly and you could run an FBA empire from a studio apartment.

Here is how FBA works for Amazon sellers.

You open up an Amazon account and you sign up for the FBA Program. Before you send items to an Amazon FBA warehouse, they have to be labeled. You'll print special barcoded labels that you'll affix to each product that you send in. They'll have to cover up any existing UPCs because when Amazon receives your items, they will scan the barcodes to identify the product as your specific inventory. Once your inventory has been received at FBA, it will be made available for sale on the Amazon website.

Amazon describes FBA this way:

With this innovative service, you send inventory directly to Amazon where it is stored and managed in a secure, climate-controlled facility. When orders are received, Amazon will professionally pick, pack and ship the product directly to your customer.

Amazon.com processes millions of orders a year while consistently ranking as one of the most trusted and highest customer satisfaction rated e-commerce companies. To maintain this unique combination, we have developed one of the most advanced online order processing and fulfillment operations in the world. From the advanced web-to-warehouse, high-speed picking and sorting system to our complete shipping carrier integration, Amazon's technology results in your customers getting what they ordered, when they ordered it.

Whether you're considering just a few items and shipments a week or millions of products and orders per year, you can put Amazon's expertise and experience to work for your business with Fulfillment by Amazon.

Put Amazon's Fulfillment Technology to Work for You.

You sell it, we ship it. Amazon has created one of the most advanced fulfillment networks in the world, and your business can now benefit from our expertise. With Fulfillment by Amazon (FBA) you store your products in Amazon's fulfillment centers, and we directly pack, ship, and provide customer service for these products.

Enjoy these benefits when you use Fulfillment by Amazon.

Eligible for FREE Super Saver Shipping & Amazon Prime

Customers love FREE Super Saver Shipping and Amazon Prime. FBA Listings on Amazon.com feature these delivery messages increasing awareness of product eligibility for free shipping.

Competitive Pricing:

Your FBA listings on Amazon.com are sorted by the item price without a shipping cost. Amazon assumes they will ship for free with FREE Super Saver Shipping or Prime, which gives you an edge when competing!

Trusted Customer Service and Returns:

FBA listings are displayed with the "Fulfillment by Amazon" logo, so customers know that packing, delivery, customer service and returns are all handled by Amazon.

Fulfill Orders from other Channels:

FBA can fulfill your orders from other sales channels from your inventory stored at an Amazon fulfillment center. You manage your inventory through a simple online user interface, and can direct us to return the inventory in our fulfillment centers at any time.

FBA Fees

There are fees that are associated with FBA. The good thing is that they are all known ahead of time and most of them are fixed. The only one that differs is the commission, as it is category specific, and it only changes if you change your price. If you sell an item for a certain price, you'll know all fees ahead of time and you'll be able to calculate your payout and determine the product's profitability (or not).

Amazon even provides a handy FBA calculator here:

https://sellercentral.amazon.com/gp/fbacalc/fba-calculator.html

You can use the FBA calculator not only to calculate expected payouts on your FBA inventory, but also to compare total fulfillment costs when deciding between using FBA for your items or keeping them for self-fulfillment.

Inbound Shipping Fee

This is the cost of getting your items to the FBA warehouse. Amazon lets you use UPS partnered shipping so you get Amazon UPS rates, which you can probably imagine are the best in the world. This is a tremendously advantageous feature of FBA that is oftentimes overlooked or taken for granted. This discounted rate can turn items that were at one point not profitable for you to sell into items that are now profitable. A 50 pound box typically ships for around $9-$15 depending on how close you are to your nearest fulfillment center. You can also arrange to ship pallets by LTL shipments (Less Than Truckload) or choose your own shipper.

Your inbound shipping fees can change if Amazon decides to change which fulfillment center your items are going to. While this can affect the profitability of your items, changes in these fees should not make or break an item in terms of overall profitability. If they do, then I suggest selling different items with higher margins.

Amazon Commission

This varies depending on the categories that you sell in.

Pick & Pack Fee

Amazon charges a fixed fee for picking and packing your orders.

Weight Based Fee

Amazon charges a weight-based fee on the outbound shipping fees. Heavier items will incur higher weight-based fees when they ship so price your items appropriately.

Storage Fee

Storage fees are very low and the first 30 days are free. You can manage your FBA inventory levels and replenish your inventory as needed to keep 30 days worth of sales in stock to prevent paying any FBA storage fees.

Even if you do end up paying storage fees, you'll find that they are very reasonable.

Long Term Storage Fee

FBA Long-Term Storage

The Long Term Storage Fee is $45/cubic foot that is charged on items stored in FBA warehouses for more than one year. This does not mean that every item that you send to FBA has to sell within 12 months. **There is an exemption for single units of any specific product.** This means that Amazon still wants your Long Tail items (items that sell, they simply don't sell very often), they just don't want three copies of a book that sells once every three years. This would be nine years supply of inventory and it is not how Amazon envisioned the FBA program.

Here are some examples of the Long Term Storage Fee on a book and a toy:

Item	Dimensions	1 unit	2nd unit	10 units
Book	8" X 6" X 1"	$0.00	$1.10	$9.90
Toy	11" X 8" X 2"	$0.00	$4.58	$41.22

Believe me, Amazon does NOT want to charge you the Long Term Storage Fee. This is not a profit center for them. They want FBA warehouses humming with inventory coming in and orders going out. This is what they are good at. They do not want to be in the storage business.

Avoiding the Long Term Storage Fee by Analyzing Your Aging Inventory

Log into your Amazon Seller Account:

https://sellercentral.amazon.com/gp/homepage.html (seller account required)

Look under Reports, and then click on Fulfillment.

Under Inventory, you'll see two reports. One called Inventory Health, and the other called Recommended Removal.

Request both of these reports to be downloaded. Save, and open in Excel. Familiarize yourself with these reports; they are very helpful. Right now you want to look at the columns that relate to Inventory Age (270-365 days & 365+ days) as this will show you the items on which Amazon will charge you the Long Term Storage Fee.

Creating a Removal Order

FBA Manual 6.4 Create Removal Orders

Amazon has actually made this process fairly easy. Here's how I did it on my accounts:

Go to your Seller Account, Reports, Fulfillment, choose Recommended Removal, View Online, click on Generate Report.

You'll now see the first 150 items from your Recommended Removal Report. These are all items that will be charged the Long Term Removal Fee or that have single quantities of inventory that have been in stock for 365+ days. Click on Begin Removal Process.

Most of these items you will want to remove or destroy. The ones to double check are the ones that have a Fulfillable Quantity of one and Available Quantity of one (even if at FBA for 365+ days). These may be Long Tail items that you want to keep in inventory. Remember, single inventory units per ASIN are exempt from the Long Term Storage Fee. I copied and pasted the ASIN into Amazon to check the prices and Sales Rank for these items to decide if I wanted to keep the items at FBA or remove/destroy them. If you want to keep them, check the box in the Delete column to remove the item from the removal order. Once you have reviewed the items, click the Continue button at the bottom of the screen and complete the process. If you have more than 150 items to review, repeat the process for the additional items.

Creating a Disposal Order

Follow the same steps as above for creating a Removal Order, but instead of clicking Ship To Address and entering an address, you'll click on Destroy. Trust me; when Amazon says they will destroy the items, they will be destroyed.

What's Really Going On?

This fee is designed to encourage FBA sellers to manage their FBA inventory better and to not simply use FBA warehouses as a cheap storage unit for their entire inventory. The FBA storage fees were so low that many sellers (myself included) simply sent Amazon everything because it was so cheap to store it at FBA that it made sense to do so.

In the fourth quarter of 2010, Amazon halted inbound FBA shipments because FBA warehouses were full. This fee will prevent this from happening again. Amazon wanted nothing but to receive inbound shipments and get stuff listed and sold, but too many sellers filled up the warehouses with slow moving inventory. The new Long Term Storage Fee will discourage this practice and keep FBA warehouses able to receive products without any delays.

Which Fulfillment Center Will My Items Go To?

This is an important question because depending on where you live geographically and the type of products that you sell, this will affect your Inbound Shipping Fees. Books & Media will go to one place and toys will go to another. Oversize items will go to another and clothing items will go to yet another. Amazon assigns the fulfillment center based on many factors. These factors include (in order):

1. Item Size (regular or oversize)
2. Amazon Category (books, tools, toys, clothes, etc.)
3. The Popularity of the Item
4. Regional Demand/Order Patterns (Amazon wants to get inventory into fulfillment centers closest to the demand to lower shipping times in transit as well as costs.
5. Current Inventory Levels
6. Seller Proximity to Fulfillment Center

So unfortunately, seller proximity to the fulfillment center is only a minor consideration. Always remember to compare the cost of paying regular UPS rates for your inbound shipping. The Amazon partnered UPS rates should be seen as an extra bonus

As a business strategy note, I would strongly suggest that if the inbound shipping rates are causing an item to not be a profitable match for FBA that you simply stop selling the product and source other, more profitable items. Cutting margins razor thin where an item is profitable if inbound shipping is $0.25/pound but not when it is $0.70/pound is not the types of margins that I recommend people play with.

Summary:

Think of it this way: only send Amazon a maximum of ONE YEAR SUPPLY of any product and you will never be charged the Long Term Storage Fee. Single quantity items are excluded so you can still send in Long Tail items without worry. Periodically check the Inventory Health Report and the Recommended Removal Report. Most FBA sellers who sell books and media items with a quantity of one will be largely unaffected by this new fee. If you need any help having your inventory returned to you or disposed of, please contact Amazon's Seller Support team using the Contact Us link in your Seller Account.

To be sure you are reviewing the most current FBA fees, always check the Amazon FBA website:

http://www.amazon.com/gp/help/customer/display.html/?nodeId=2002 42950

Pricing Your FBA Items

There are additional fees associated with FBA, but you will also sell your items for a higher price so in most cases you will actually receive a higher net payout per transaction even though you have additional transaction fees. This would seem impossible considering the fact that by using FBA you are also doing less work and you are keeping your customers happier by providing faster shipping services than you could provide yourself. Much more on how to price FBA items later in the book.

Return Policy

Amazon handles customer service for all FBA orders. Amazon is very conscientious about keeping their customers happy. They will allow a customer to return an item for pretty much any reason. This opens the door for abuse sometimes and there are instances where a customer can take advantage of this policy at the expense of your inventory.

If you find that you are receiving a higher return rate on an item that is affecting your target margins, you will have to evaluate the item's compatibility with FBA. You can raise your price to compensate or you can try to sell the item on other channels and ship your orders from your FBA inventory using Multi-Channel Fulfillment (more in Chapter 21). You may even decide that the product is no longer a good match for FBA and you can request that Amazon return the products to you.

International Orders

Currently, Amazon will ship your books and media items internationally for you at no extra charge (customer pays shipping). To sell your books and media items internationally, you need to add this service to your Amazon seller account (free) and then upload a digital copy of your signature that Amazon will use on export documents and customs forms. If you sell items from other categories on Amazon, they will not be eligible for international shipping (through Amazon direct sales or Multi-Channel Fulfillment). I would expect that Amazon would offer this service in the future.

Amazon as a Competitor

When selling on Amazon using FBA, you may enjoy a time of being the only FBA seller for an item. This is an ideal situation but it doesn't always last. Other sellers can convert their inventory to FBA and start to drive the price down. Sometimes you may be selling an item that Amazon does not currently carry and have a type of exclusivity. In the event that Amazon starts to carry these products directly, they may be able to sell them at lower margins than you are comfortable with. In cases like this, you can try to sell your items on other channels and fulfill any orders using Multi-Channel Fulfillment. You can do this until you are sold out of inventory, or you can even request to have your inventory removed and returned to you. Then re-evaluate the item considering your costs and profit margin goals and decide if it is still a good match to sell online. There is a bonus section at the end of this book with strategies for competing with Amazon as a seller.

Unfulfillable Inventory

If a customer returns an item, Amazon will determine if the item can be resold or not. If it can be resold, it will be added to your existing FBA inventory. If not, it will be marked as 'unfulfillable' and you will have to request that it be returned to you or destroyed. Best Practice is to remove your entire unfulfillable inventory once a month or so. You may find that items were damaged or that there was nothing wrong with your items. Just reprocess them to your FBA account if they are still in sellable condition. Amazon can also automate this process for you and send your unfulfillable inventory back to you on a regular schedule.

Downsides of FBA

Even with all the positive things that FBA allows sellers to do, there are some things to keep in mind when deciding if you are going to send all or some of your inventory to an FBA warehouse. FBA has the power to transform your business overnight, but it is important to know how it all works and the potential risks involved when handing over a significant portion of your business process to another company.

You Lose Control Over Your Order Processing

You are handing over all aspects of order processing to Amazon. You are trusting them to store, pick, pack, and ship your items. This can be a scary thought for some sellers who take great pride in providing their customers with a high quality shipping process. You may decide to only send certain items to FBA and keep higher valued items or items that would require special packaging at your location to ship yourself.

You Hand Over Customer Service to Amazon

Amazon will handle all customer service issues on your FBA orders. This means that you lose control of the returns process (a customer can return an item without approval from you, the seller). It is possible (although unlikely) that a buyer abuses this liberal return policy at the expense of your inventory. If you suspect anything like this, report it to Amazon. They monitor excessive customer returns as well as A-Z Guarantee claims.

Possibility of Loss or Damage to Your Products

It is possible that your items are lost or damaged either by UPS on the way to Amazon or by Amazon themselves, but that same risk is there for every item dropped off at the post office. Amazon will reimburse sellers for lost or damaged items automatically. It is important to monitor your inbound items as they are received. Amazon will send an email if there are any problems receiving your items.

Items not good for FBA

Unfortunately, FBA is not perfect for every type of item. Here are some items that I would be cautious to send to FBA as well as the reasons why.

Low Margin Items

If you have low margins, then one or two returns can wipe out all profitability on the entire product. Returns are inevitable and the cost of returns should be factored into your expected margin on every item that you sell.

High Fraud Categories

Categories that can be more susceptible to fraud and abuse are computers and electronics. Because Amazon handles the customer service, fraudulent buyers may try to take advantage of the generous return policy. Consider this when deciding what to send to FBA. FBA still works in these categories, but a buyer looking to take advantage of Amazon is more likely going to do so over an iPad than over a shower curtain. Amazon monitors buyers just like they monitor sellers. Buyers can also be kicked off of Amazon.

Expensive Items

Use your own discretion when considering sending high-dollar items to FBA. While they do enjoy the same boost that you will get for all FBA items by attracting Amazon's best customers, they will also be open to fraud and return policy abuse. This just makes more work for you to do if you have to track extra returns and inspect the items more carefully. An expensive return can hurt a lot more than an inexpensive one.

Collectible Items

Amazon is not currently the optimal sales channel for one-of-a-kind collectibles. EBay is still the best place for these types of items. I know exactly how Amazon could add this category through FBA, but that's the subject of another book.

When considering these types of items, consider the overall impact of the item on your sales. If you receive additional returns on an item, do those returns negatively impact the OVERALL profitability of that product over a period of time? Run the numbers for a few months to get a good sample of sales. If you sell ten of an item a month when you fulfill your own orders, but twenty per month through FBA, are the overall additional sales worth any increase in returns? If yes, send to FBA. If not, don't send to FBA.

FBA is a very powerful program and if used correctly, will greatly improve your margins, profits, and efficiency. It can give you back your time to focus on other parts of your business such as sourcing products or just spending more time with your family.

Types of Amazon Seller Accounts

There are primarily two types of seller accounts on Amazon.

Sell Your Stuff (Formerly Individual Account)

You can start selling on Amazon with absolutely no fees. There is no fee to have an Sell Your Stuff Account to list items for sale. You pay fees when your items sell. These fees will include a Per Transaction Fee of $0.99/item. You cannot create new product pages, set your own shipping charges, or use specific data feeds and upload methods if you only have an Sell Your Stuff Account.

Sell Professionally (Formerly Pro Merchant Account)

If you are running a arbitrage business, then you will most likely want to sign up for a Sell Professionally Account. The cost is $39.95/month. You can then create new product pages and set your own shipping rates. You also get access to many additional reports as well as the ability to feed data and files directly to your seller account. A Sell Professionally Account is required to use many third-party listing tools like ScanPower for this reason.

Sell Professionally Account do not pay the $0.99 Per Transaction Fee that Sell Your Stuff Account sellers pay on every item. So as long as you sell 40 items a month, a Sell Professionally account is basically free. If you sell hundreds of items per month, then having a Sell Professionally Account will actually save you a ton of money.

If you are just starting out and you don't know which account to sign up for, remember the tipping point of selling 40 items per month means a Sell Professionally Account is basically free. Follow the principles laid out in this book and selling 40 items per month will not be an issue. It may be a good strategy to not sign up for an Amazon seller account until you have acquired enough inventory to list to support a sales volume of 40 items per month. Remember, that's just over one order per day.

A lot of this book will focus on FBA, but you do not need to use FBA to fulfill your Amazon orders. You can sell on Amazon and ship yourself, although once you use FBA, even one order a day can seem like a huge inconvenience. The same economic principles of supply, demand, price, and margin will apply; you'll just be shipping your own orders.

So now that you know what FBA is, let's explain WHY FBA works so well.

Chapter 4 – Why Does FBA Work?

So why does FBA work? There are many reasons that FBA works and works well, but the thing to consider is that FBA works all around; it works for sellers as well as for buyers. It also works for Amazon.

FBA for Sellers

For starters, FBA sellers enjoy many competitive advantages over their non-FBA competitors known as merchant fulfilled sellers. Many of these advantages are listed below:

FBA sellers have a greater probability of winning the Buy Box, even without being the lowest price.

FBA sellers can win the New and Used Buy Boxes in the Books, Music, Videos, and DVD categories.

FBA sellers are listed first on the offers pages, even if selling for the same net price (price + shipping).

FBA sellers get their items marketed on the Amazon.com website with guaranteed delivery dates.

FBA works because it puts your inventory on the same level as Amazon's own inventory and markets it to Amazon's best customers. Amazon's customers are smart; they know what they want and they trust Amazon. Amazon buyers pay more for the exact same item in order to get it from Amazon rather than from a third party seller. Why? Isn't it the same item? The same item, yes, but buyers are buying more than just the item. They are buying the customer service, they are buying the return policy, and they are buying the order fulfillment process. For these reasons, buyers will pay more to get their items from Amazon or an FBA seller than they will to get their items from a third party seller who ships their own orders. Consider Amazon Prime members (explained in more detail below) who get free 2-Day Air shipping on everything that they buy as long as it ships from Amazon or an FBA seller. Buyers choose FBA sellers over merchant fulfilled sellers over and over again, willingly, very willingly.

Consider an item that ships fast and free by UPS 2-Day Air for Amazon Prime members compared to the same item for the same price from a merchant fulfilled seller who ships by USPS Parcel Post or Media Mail for books. At the same price, it's a no-brainer. Even at a higher price, the fast shipping is such a value that many buyers are happy to pay a little more (sometimes a lot more) to get the same item faster.

We'll talk more about understanding the Amazon customer in the next chapter, but first we need to talk about a huge piece of the FBA success puzzle and that is Amazon's free shipping programs. They are called Amazon Prime and Free Super Saver Shipping (FSSS).

Amazon Prime

Amazon Prime is brilliant. Amazon Prime members pay $79/year and in return receive free 2-Day Air shipping on everything that they buy on Amazon (did you know that 79 is a PRIME number?). This applies to all items sold by Amazon and through FBA sellers. There are rare exceptions for items that do not qualify for Amazon Prime, but they are so rare that I have not even seen one recently enough to put in here as an example. Amazon Prime members can also choose to pay $3.99 for Overnight shipping on any item.

Think about that. **This is powerful stuff!** Even if you, personally, don't find this service useful, you can bet that a ton of Amazon buyers do. I know I'm one of them! We buy practically everything we can from Amazon, and often at the best price. Getting it delivered free in two days (sometimes next day) is just an extra bonus.

Amazon Prime Program Details; Amazon.com/prime

Unlimited FREE 2-day shipping on all eligible orders – You don't have to order that much from Amazon to get a lot of value out of this program. Even one package a month would cost you more to request 2-Day shipping than the $7/month for Amazon Prime.

No minimum purchase required for free shipping – Even a $5 pair of scissors will be at your door in two days for free if you're an Amazon Prime member. Are you really going to drive to the store just for scissors?

Send gifts across the continental US at no additional cost – You don't just have to ship to your house. You can have Amazon ship birthday gifts, wedding gifts, or Christmas gifts right up to the last minute, all free.

Add up to four accounts in your household to your account – Just about anyone in your house can use Amazon Prime and get things delivered free in two days.

Get overnight shipping for only $3.99 per item

Seriously? $3.99 to send just about anything overnight? Order today, at your house tomorrow for under $4. I'm not driving halfway across town over $4 unless I absolutely have to have the item tonight (which is pretty rare). You can get DVDs, toothpaste, cereal, and diapers, all at your door the next day for under $4. Can you see how a buyer could get used to this? Did The Weather Channel just forecast a hurricane in your area next week? Just order your generator from Amazon and get it delivered TOMORROW for $3.99. Yes, even some heavy generators ship overnight from Amazon for $3.99.

Amazon actively promotes and markets their shipping capabilities (and items that qualify)

Amazon will even tell you on the product page how much time you have left if you want the item delivered tomorrow or the next day using two day shipping. Depending on where the Amazon fulfillment center is located, 2-Day Air shipments can often arrive overnight.

Here's how this works in practice: say I want to order the Kindle. I can order it as late as 6:30 CST and for $3.99 it will be at my door tomorrow at about 10:30. If I can wait an extra day, it's free. This is powerful stuff. Forgot your anniversary is tomorrow? Order in the afternoon and it's delivered the next morning.

(Shipping and delivery times will vary by individual, but we get our UPS shipments around 10:30 AM)

More and more Amazon customers are becoming Amazon Prime members. This will mean more and more customers who begin to value the fast, free shipping services that Amazon Prime members enjoy on every order. Amazon has several programs that introduce Amazon buyers to Amazon Prime with free trials such as Amazon Moms and Amazon Students.

As an extra bonus, Amazon Prime members get access to the entire Amazon Prime Instant Videos catalog. Not really related to selling on Amazon, but I mention it here to show you that Amazon is pushing Amazon Prime to more and more of their customers. The more Amazon Prime members there are, the more attractive items listed by FBA sellers will become versus items listed by merchant fulfilled sellers. The demand for the products will stay the same, but the number of purchases will continue to shift towards the FBA sellers and away from the merchant fulfilled sellers. Whose side do you want to be on?

Free Super Saver Shipping

This is another genius Amazon business model. As long as you buy $35 worth of items or more, you get free shipping! Partner this with no tax and the delivered price often beats the local price on many items. Free

Super Saver Shipping is not as fast as Amazon Prime and orders don't always ship right away, but they do ship for free and this is all that matters for many cost conscious buyers. It also encourages buyers to add additional items to their shopping carts prior to checkout to get over that magical $35 mark and get the free shipping. Now consider this: a buyer has $21 in their shopping cart and wants to get FSSS so they start looking for something that they need for around $14. They find an item that should work and they look at the offers. If you are the only FBA offer at $14, then they have to choose you because the item has to be from Amazon or from an FBA seller. It's actually less expensive for them to add your $14 FBA item and get FSSS than to checkout at $21 and pay for shipping. As for your merchant fulfilled competition on that $14 item, they are not even being considered because their inventory is not eligible for FSSS at all!

Earlier we briefly talked about how FBA sellers are able to make more money on each item by using FBA than if they fulfilled their online orders themselves. They can do this despite the additional FBA fees that they pay. You may be thinking that this doesn't make sense; how can a seller pay more fees, yet make more per sale? That's what I'll explain here with some examples. Understanding this part of FBA is very important. FBA items are priced much differently than regular merchant fulfilled items. Pricing your FBA inventory optimally is an art form itself because you are not limited to simply competing on price.

How Sellers Should Price FBA Items

Learning how to price FBA items is one of the most important things that you need to master. This is important for two reasons. First, you don't want to price too low and leave a ton of margin and profit on the table for no reason. Second, you don't want to price too high and miss out on sales. In the next chapter, we'll talk about Understanding The Amazon Customer and why they will often pay more for items sold by FBA sellers. For now, let's stick to the basics of pricing FBA items against merchant fulfilled items.

So if you aren't supposed to be the lowest price and you're not supposed to be the highest price, then how should I price? Good question! Unfortunately there is no perfect answer for how to price FBA items. I'll give you some guidelines as to when to price aggressively as well as when to command a premium price over your merchant fulfilled competition.

The first thing to remember is that your FBA inventory is eligible for Amazon's free shipping programs. This is very important. This means that your listing on a product's offers page will be sorted by the total 'net price', meaning price plus shipping. If you are selling a book and the lowest price from a merchant fulfilled seller is $5 + $3.99 shipping and you price your book at $5 as an FBA seller, then sure, your offer will show first as the lowest price, but you just priced yourself $3.99 LOWER than the already lowest net price. By default, if you want to be the lowest price as an FBA seller against merchant fulfilled offers, then you should be matching their net price. In this case it would be $8.99. So even though your price is $8.99 and their price is $5, you would show first on the offers page because FBA is the tiebreaker. Amazon buyers are smart and they will compare apples to apples and see the total 'shipped' price in their shopping carts. Unless you have a really good reason, such as all merchant fulfilled sellers being listed at artificially high prices, you should not be pricing any of your items below the lowest merchant fulfilled 'net price'.

This comes back to Win #1 discussed earlier in this book where sellers will get higher total payouts on the exact same item when using FBA instead of processing orders themselves. They are able to sell at a higher price so even though they have additional fees associated with using FBA, these additional fees are covered by the increase in sales price. Of course, this is all in addition to not actually having to ship all of your own orders!

Here are two strategies that you can take when pricing your items: The Fast Nickel vs. The Slow Dime.

The Fast Nickel is when you price aggressively in order to get a fast sale. There is a value in getting paid fast. You are able to get in, get paid, and get out. The risk that you took by purchasing the item for resale is gone. Sometimes you may sell for a price lower than what the buyer was willing to pay, but you accept that price for the fast sale and lower risk compared to holding onto the item and trying to get a higher price.

The Slow Dime means that you price yourself a little higher than your competition and you market yourself as a premium seller to the buyer. Higher prices, higher margins, higher profits. You may simply be pricing higher as an FBA seller just waiting for a buyer who puts a higher value on fast, free shipping. If you are holding your items for longer periods of time, you do expose yourself to risks such as price erosion or market price drops. It could be a weaker future demand for the product, which would lower price, or increased competition that would increase supply and bring down price. When this happens, suddenly that quick sale, or Fast Nickel, even at a lower price, starts to look attractive.

Different products will deserve different strategies. You may have to experiment with different strategies on different items. One thing to always remember: if an item sells too fast, it's priced too low. If it takes too long to sell, then it's priced too high (these rules do not apply to Long Tail items that are not as price sensitive). A Long Tail book that only sells twice a year is going to sell twice a year regardless of price (within reason). Long Tail items do not sell on price so lowering price on Long Tail items is not a strategy that I recommend. The item will sell twice a year at $100 or at $20. Lowering your price to $20 to try to attract the sale is only going to cut into your margins. The buyer is more than happy to pay you only $20, but they would also be happy to pay $100.

Pricing Against Your Competition

Depending on what you sell, there will be different market dynamics that you have to consider when pricing your items. Amazon has New, Used, and Collectible conditions. They also have the dynamic of Amazon as a seller and third party sellers. Third party sellers have the added dynamic of some using FBA and some being merchant fulfilled. Deciding exactly how to price means that you have to consider your competition as well as the products that you are selling.

If you sell toys and you only sell toys in New condition, then you need to look at the Amazon price (if Amazon sells the item), your competition in New condition, and then if there are any FBA sellers.

If you sell books, you need to look at the Amazon price (if Amazon sells the book), the listed prices in New and Used condition, as well as if there are any FBA sellers. Even if you are selling Used books, you have to look at the New prices because sometimes you're going to see a Used book going for $30, the same book in New condition for $20, and to make it even worse, Amazon selling it for $14.95. How does this happen? Sellers who are not paying attention! They are pricing their Used books against their Used competition and not considering the entire competitive marketplace.

As an FBA seller, you can't just look at the FBA competition, either. You'll see items where merchant fulfilled sellers are all charging $25 for an item and an FBA seller at a price of $250. I know we talked about how Amazon buyers will pay a premium for FBA items, but there is a limit. I want to teach you to be more realistic when commanding a premium for your FBA items. Who knows, maybe that seller will find someone who puts a huge value on FBA, and if they do, good for them! It may also be a simple typo of an extra zero on the end of their price.

When you are the only FBA seller on an item, you are able to command a premium price, especially if Amazon does not sell the item. You will be the only seller who is able to offer the item with free 2-Day Air shipping to Amazon Prime members. There is a whole chapter later in this book about not chasing the next sale. What this means in a nutshell is that not all buyers are the same. Some will buy on price and some want fast, free shipping. Relax on price and let the buyers make their buying decisions.

Will the next buyer for this item put a high value on FBA? Maybe, but maybe not. Maybe they are buying on price. That's OK; you sit and wait for the FBA buyers. Your margins will thank you ☺

Being the only FBA offer leads me into this next phenomenon, The FBA Land Grab.

The FBA Land Grab

A land grab is generally defined as the acquisition of valuable or strategic territory for much less than its actual worth.

So what is the FBA land grab?

Amazon sellers are actively seeking out and targeting items that Amazon does not offer directly and where there are no competing FBA offers. They know that they will be able to capture sales easily and often at a higher price than the current competition. They can reach sellers whose needs are currently not met by the current list of third party sellers. Customers like Amazon Prime members, and customers who are looking for items to qualify for Free Super Saver Shipping on orders over $35. Also, customers who just don't trust third party sellers yet and prefer to have Amazon's customer service and A-to-Z Guarantee backing their purchases.

These sellers know that there is a group of Amazon buyers who are not always interested in the lowest price offer. They have other factors that influence their buying decision other than price. Things like shipping speed and customer service.

I heard from Amazon that over half of all Amazon customers have never purchased from a third party merchant who doesn't use FBA. Why not? There are several reasons including slower shipping times and unknown customer service. Using FBA can effectively double your customer base overnight.

Amazon customers want the safety, security, and speedy shipping that they know they will get from items processed by Amazon. They know they'll get great customer service should they need it and they are willing to pay more for that.

But Don't All Customers Shop Based on Price? No Way.

Will the lowest priced seller get all the sales? Nope. They'll still get some sales, but remember, price says something. There are plenty of people who simply will not buy from the lowest priced seller for the sole reason that they are the lowest price. Someone has to be the lowest priced brain surgeon, and they'll get some customers, but do you think everyone is choosing their brain surgeon based on price? Not a chance, and it's the same way with every transaction on Amazon. The low price sellers will get some sales and that's OK. It's not about volume; it's about margin (whole chapter on margin later). The FBA seller won't get all the sales either, but their sales will be more profitable and allow them to stop playing the losing game of 'Let's Lower Price To See Who Can Make The Least Amount Of Money'.

FBA sellers are able to cater to these specific smart and savvy customers who know what they want and are willing to pay for it. It's about working smart, not hard.

That's a lot of information about Why FBA Works for Amazon sellers, but while this is a book for sellers, it is important to consider why FBA works for the Amazon buyer as well.

FBA for Buyers

FBA for buyers works very well. Amazon buyers, especially Amazon Prime members, get very used to free 2-Day Air shipping on every item that they order from Amazon, including even small, inexpensive items. Until FBA came along, buyers who wanted to take advantage of the Amazon Prime shipping program were limited to only purchasing items sold by Amazon directly. If they wanted something that was not sold by Amazon but sold by a third party seller, they were at the mercy of that seller's shipping policies. This would cause some buyers to simply not purchase the item or look for other alternatives.

Now that so many more items are available through the Amazon fulfillment network from sellers utilizing the FBA program, buyers have more confidence to purchase from third party sellers. They get the depth of product selection as well as the confidence that comes from purchasing from Amazon.com. Maybe you have caught yourself looking for FBA items yourself. You find a book that you really want and you really hope that there is an FBA seller at a good price because you want your book in two days for free rather than wait on a Media Mail package to travel across the country. I know I have; I'll happily pay more for an identical item in order to get it from an FBA seller.

FBA for Amazon

Does FBA work for Amazon? You better believe it!

FBA has been a huge success for Amazon.com. It has allowed them to greatly expand their product selection through third party sellers. At the time of this writing, third party sales were responsible for 39% of Amazon's revenue (2012). That's a big chunk! Much of this growth can be attributed to FBA. It gets the depth of selection available from third party sellers in front of Amazon's best customers who have come to trust Amazon for all of their online shopping needs. I believe FBA to still be in its infancy in terms of the scope of its use and the ways in which it can be leveraged. Game Changer is not a strong enough way to describe FBA.

Chapter 5 – Understanding the Amazon Customer

When selling on Amazon (whether you are using FBA or not), it is vitally important to understand the Amazon customer. **This one piece of information alone will drastically increase your margins and profits**. It is the key to learning how to price your items on Amazon, and especially when using FBA. Learning to understand the Amazon Customer and knowing what factors they consider when making purchases will change the way that you see Amazon as a marketplace.

To start, remember this: Amazon is crazy about customer service! They have built their business on customer service. They have the best customer service, return policies, and consistently go above and beyond to keep the customer happy and make them customers for life. They have shipping programs that ensure that their customers get their orders quickly and if there are ever any problems, Amazon is there to keep the customer happy.

Amazon has said that almost half of their entire customer base has never bought from a third party merchant who doesn't use FBA. This should immediately show you that Amazon customers prefer to buy from Amazon and FBA sellers, and that price is not always the most important factor in making a buying decision.

Think of it this way; if you put all of Amazon's customers in one group, that group would have different sub-groups. These sub-groups have different characteristics as to what factors they consider most important when making a buying decision. For some, it's price. For others it's a good return policy. **For many, it's if the items are eligible for Free Super Saver Shipping and Amazon Prime.** These groups may not even make sense to you, but don't worry, they don't have to. You don't have to know why a buyer is willing to pay more for an identical item from Amazon or an FBA seller than from a third party merchant at a lower price. You just have to understand that a large portion of Amazon customers put a high value on

Amazons' shipping speed and customer service, not price. Just don't think that they don't know what they are doing. They are likely the savviest buyers on Amazon. **They know what they want, they know when they want it, and they are willing to pay for it.** They put a value on shipping speed and will actively seek out and patronize sellers whose products are eligible for the shipping speeds and customer service that they prefer. Amazon even lets buyers sort the offers pages by sellers who use FBA.

The sub-group that you need to understand is the one that seeks out Amazon and FBA offers because they want their items fast and are willing to pay more for the Amazon-backed customer service. **These are the buyers to which you are marketing yourself (and your items).**

Here is another way to look at it. Take 100 Amazon customers. Half, 50, have never bought from a third party merchant who doesn't use FBA. So for a specific item, you could have Amazon selling at $20 and a third party merchant selling for $10 + $5 shipping, or $15. There are 50 people paying $5, or 33%, more for the same item. But are the items the same? Not at all; the physical product may be the same, but the other factors surrounding this product and sale are very different. One order ships and arrives in two days for free. The other order takes 10 days to arrive. One can be returned no questions asked. The other gives the customer a runaround on returns.

To understand this sub-group of Amazon customers, you need to fully understand Amazons' shipping programs that were discussed in the last chapter, Amazon Prime and Free Super Saver Shipping.

When you use FBA, all of your items are eligible for these same shipping promotions and Amazon customers who value the shipping speed will buy from you, even if at a higher price.

Customers do want a good price and often Amazon does have the best price. Buying from Amazon is often a no-brainer because of the best price, no tax (for most), and free shipping. As long as you don't absolutely need the item today, then it often makes more sense to buy the item from Amazon than from a local retailer. This applies to all Amazon orders that ship for free, but more so for Amazon Prime members who will get their items in just two days. Amazon customers will frequently spend more on the same item to get it from Amazon than from another online retailer, even a local store. Why? There are many reasons. You could say, "What's wrong with them? They could go buy it on eBay for less!" Maybe, but some Amazon buyers may absolutely hate eBay and refuse to even look there. They may be very busy and not have time to shop different sites and local stores just to save a few bucks. They may not live near a local store that carries what they need. They may not even have a car to go shopping! **The fact is, they know what they want, they know when they want it, and they are willing to pay for it.** What these buyers want are items that use Amazon's fulfillment network so that they get them fast.

Examples where price is not the deciding factor

Deadlines

How about birthdays, holidays, anniversaries? These are set on the calendar and if you want to order something online and get it in time, you have to plan ahead. UPS Ground and Media Mail aren't exactly the faster things around in terms of delivery times. When it's two days before Christmas and you're still shopping on Amazon, your options are limited as to which items can still be delivered on time. If you're using FBA, your items can get there in time while your competition simply cannot deliver (at any price).

Or think of it this way; you're going on a cruise in two days and you want to take a specific book with you. That third party merchant offer simply will not arrive in time but that FBA sellers' item will. You are not upset that you had to pay more than the lowest price. You are thankful that the book was available to you at a price you were willing to pay and you're able to take it with you on the cruise!

They just want the item fast and will pay a few bucks more to get it

This happens all the time. It's simply a matter of 'time is money'. Most book and media sellers use USPS Media Mail for their shipments. This can take up to two weeks to arrive. Don't you think that Prime member is just going to pay more to get the same item in two days? There is a value in getting the item sooner. Will everyone pay to get it faster? No. Some will wait months to save $0.50, but those aren't the customers you're looking for. You're selling to different customers. **They know what they want, when they want it, and are willing to pay for it.**

Chapter 6 – Economics of Supply, Demand, & Price

The only thing that sets PRICE in the reseller, or secondary market, is SUPPLY and DEMAND.

You probably remember something about supply and demand from high school economics. Personally, I find the economics of arbitrage and resale to be fascinating. There are some key points of supply, demand, and price that all resellers should know.

First thing to remember is that different buyers place a different value on the exact same item. Different buyers will place a different personal, internal value on any item that they purchase. Think of it like this: when a buyer buys an item, only they know how much they actually value that item. They value that $10 item for AT LEAST $10 (or else they would not buy it), but probably not exactly $10 (meaning that they would not buy it if priced at $10.01). They may be willing to pay up to $12, or even $20. If they had a starving baby at home and it was the last package of baby food, they may put an exceedingly high value on the product!

You don't see this personal, internal value because the prices are set at the store for all customers. They all pay the same price at retail stores even though we know that some buyers place a higher value on each and every purchase. When this is played out online where prices are set by the resellers who have a limited supply of any particular item, it becomes much more evident that some buyers are willing to pay more for a product than the Manufacturer's Suggested Retail Price (MSRP).

Second is that supply, demand, and price are always changing. Each time you look at an item, you are looking at a snapshot in time where price has been set based on supply and demand. As time goes by, the dynamics change. Demand will go up if the product gets increased advertising or demand can go down if it receives poor user reviews. Supply can go up if the manufacturer is able to make more, or supply can go down as buyers buy the items and remove sellable quantity from the marketplace. Price will change accordingly with changes in supply and demand.

I want you to consider one more dynamic at play here. In addition to price, supply, and demand, I want you to add the concept of TIME. We are dealing with the Amazon marketplace at specific moments in time. As time goes by, things will change. When resellers find a deal, and they list their inventory on Amazon.com, this increases the supply on Amazon. The overall supply does not change. That supply used to be for sale at Target and now it is for sale on Amazon.com. So now that the Amazon.com supply has increased, the Amazon.com price will decrease. As time goes by, buyers will buy items and sellers will sell items. How does this affect the overall picture? As sellers sell, their supply goes down. Depending on the product, demand may stay constant, or even increase while supply is dropping. This will of course affect price. Sellers won't have an unlimited supply of their products. As they sell out at whatever price they are charging, they will stop being competitors.

This spike in supply is local to the Amazon marketplace and it is a temporary spike. This means that the decrease in price is a temporary decrease.

You can also consider using a 'Buy & Hold' strategy when you see this unfold on an item that you are selling. Buy an item at a hot price, but hold onto it while other sellers complete and drive the price down. Once their supply is gone, the price often returns to it's original level.

Another strategy to consider is using Multi-Channel Fulfillment (covered in depth in Chapter 21). You can use Multi-Channel Fulfillment to fulfill orders at profitable prices from other sales channels if you find the temporarily lowered Amazon.com price to not be at a profitable level.

Price Gouging

If you do this long enough, you may run into someone who thinks that resellers are price-gouging consumers and that items should never be sold for more than their original listed price or MSRP. I find this idea to be preposterous. As mentioned earlier in this chapter, price is set by supply and demand, nothing more. This is a free market where buyers and sellers are free to make transactions if both parties agree to the terms. This is how each and every transaction occurs every day. When someone buys a product, they are saying that they value that product for more than they value that amount of cash in their pocket. The store or seller values that amount of cash in their register more than they value that product on their shelf. If neither one of these conditions are met, then the transaction would not take place. It is not as evident at retail stores where prices are fixed for all customers, but certain customers will value different items for more or less than other buyers. This applies to all products, even milk! Say milk is $3/gallon. Some people place a personal value on milk so close to the listed price that they would not buy milk if the price went up by 25 cents. Some buyers would buy milk even if it jumped to $10/gallon! Even though both buyers can buy milk for $3/gallon, one buyer places a higher personal value on the purchase. The store prices milk at the equilibrium price related to supply and demand to maximize their profits through price and quantity sold. If they raised their price to $10/gallon, they would still sell some, but they would not sell as much. So even though they have a higher price and margin per item, they lose out on so many sales that the price is not justified.

Consider when items go into short supply. How about after a hurricane when demand for generators and chainsaws spikes. Stores like Home Depot don't raise their prices, but it creates a shortage because demand outweighs the limited supply. An individual who is not bound by any agreements (the way that Home Depot is) is free to sell their spare generator on the open market for any price that they are able to get. The generator may have been purchased for $500, but they could put it on

Craigslist for $2000. Because of the high demand and low supply, price goes up. What if there had been no hurricane? Would the buyer be able to get $2000? Of course not! Any buyer could just go to Home Depot and purchase one off the shelf. It's a difference of not just price, but availability. Home Depot selling at a price of $500 on a generator is not much use if they are not in stock.

So who is the buyer who pays $2000 for a $500 generator? The buyer who places a personal value of $2000 (or more) on having a generator today rather than in a few weeks when Home Depot gets more in stock. They are paying a premium but they are able to enjoy the utility of the product during a period of time when it was not attainable at the price point of $500. This is not price gouging; this is price being set by supply and demand at any single point in time with all external factors considered. Even at a price of $2000, there may be demand at an even higher price. The seller may sell for $2000 only to get a call with an offer for $2500 or $3000.

Items go into short supply for many reasons. This happens every year with popular toys.

There was a post on an online message board by someone who thought that anyone selling toys on Amazon for more than their MSRP was price gouging. Here was my response:

We live in a world with many dynamics. If someone wants a hot, popular item (any item, not just toys) then they may have to pay a premium if they are sold out everywhere. MSRP doesn't do much good at Toys R Us if they are sold out. Their alternative? Wait until SUPPLY catches up with DEMAND and lowers PRICE.

PRICE, SUPPLY, and DEMAND are all constant at any point in time on any marketplace. They will all change over time. This is the market at work. PRICE too high? Only reasons are either high DEMAND or low SUPPLY. In this case, more SUPPLY will enter the market, and PRICE will come down. As people buy, DEMAND will go down, and so will PRICE. The people who buy when PRICE is high are the ones who value the item the most. People value identical items differently. MSRP is not the value of the item to all people. The only time a buyer buys something is because they value the item MORE than they value the money in their pocket. How much more? That varies by individual. If they did not value the item more than the money in their pocket, then they would not buy the item. This is how all buying decisions are made.

A toy at Toys R Us can be $25 but out of stock. Their price is still $25; you just can't buy it. On Amazon it may be $50, but IN STOCK. That's the difference.

You're forgetting the buyers who are THANKFUL that resellers, through Amazon or another sales channel, are able to get the items available for sale on the open market. They are happy that they are able to get what they want for a price that they are willing to pay. If they were not willing to pay it, they would not purchase the item. Some pay for convenience, some may value the item for even more than the sales price.

Think of someone who spends their time driving around town to track down a hard to find (short supply) toy and they find some. They offer them for sale online. It's the toy that I want and know it's hard to find I would rather pay a premium for the toy and be done with the purchase and not have to drive all over town shopping (and possibly not even find the toy). Not everyone would put this value on an item, but some will. Some people put an extreme value on their time and will happily spend money in order to save their time. Again, not everyone does, but some do. It's a free market where buyers and sellers are able to make transactions when both sides believe they are attaining the greater value.

Here's an example; my favorite style of sunglasses is not made anymore. Personally, I will pay more for this style than other people will. I found them on eBay for a fair price, but I would have paid EVEN MORE. If the price were higher, I would still have bought them. I was happy to buy them for the sellers' price. Some people would say that I got ripped off buying old model sunglasses for above MSRP. It's my choice and I am thankful that the seller still had old stock and through the Internet, we are able to make a transaction.

You know that feeling where you got a 'deal'? Where you found something that you wanted and were able to get it for a lot less than you expected to pay? The seller was happy with the price that you paid or else you would not have made a transaction. You were willing to pay more but you got a deal. It may not have been a deal to everyone (and that's OK), but it was a deal to you.

Remember the original Tickle Me Elmo (1996)? People were posting classified ads in the paper since there was no Craigslist, eBay, or Amazon marketplace. Amazon, eBay and other online sites actually bring prices down as close to equilibrium as possible based on supply and demand. The supply is constant at any point in time. Thanks to the Internet, more of that supply can be made available. SUPPLY and DEMAND are the only things that determine PRICE.

I believe most people who complain about this practice are misdirecting their own frustration at themselves for not doing it themselves and making money in the process. Where's the proof? If they really wanted to, they could buy the same hot toys and resell them at cost or MSRP to all the people that they think they are protecting. They will quickly see that the time and effort surrounding a reseller is not 'free'. They'll run into buyers who are willing to pay more, but will happily pay less. They may even sell to a reseller.

Chapter 7 – The History of Scouting

A brief history on mobile scouting: How did this all get started?

When Amazon started to allow booksellers to sell their books on their site, a powerful new sales channel emerged. Anyone, anywhere could start to sell his or her books online. This was something new and powerful. You could see the price at which other sellers were selling an item for and gauge an item's value. **Selling books on Amazon became popular because they were easy!** They were easy to find cheap (thrift stores, book sales), easy to check/list (barcodes), easy to store (size), and easy to ship (Media Mail).

The first book scouters would go to book sales and grab as many books as they could that they thought would be valuable. Then go to a corner and call a friend at home and read them the ISBN or UPC. Their friend would then enter the number in Amazon.com and relay back if the book was good or not. This left the library sales with piles of discarded books in the corners of their rooms. If you have ever been to a sale where they say you have to buy 90% of what you pull, this is why. Believe It or not, I still see people doing this and I can only guess they are trying to save the monthly fee associated with a scouting service but it seems terribly inefficient to me.

Technology gradually evolved to allow sellers to come in with Internet connected laptops and use their cell phones to look up items. This was at a time where mobile data speeds were slow; no 3G or 4G back then! Looking up prices live was not efficient and the local database system was born. Companies would compile Amazon pricing data into a database that worked with a PDA and laser scanner. Local database solutions would show you the title, Sales Rank, and the lowest available prices for an item. You would then make the decision whether you should buy that item. It was the best solution at the time, and still is a viable solution if you often scout where there is no wireless data connection or Wi-Fi (although places like this are becoming fewer and farther between).

Local database services thrived for a few years. When FBA came along, I think they all underestimated the enormous change that was happening on the Amazon marketplace. None of these services were displaying FBA offers (or lack thereof). They were all focused on books and media items only when many FBA sellers quickly realized that they could buy and sell practically anything. The local database services simply did not meet the changing needs of Amazon sellers who were using the FBA platform.

Local database systems are also limited to 2 GB of pricing data or less due to hardware limitations of Windows Mobile PDAs. FBA sellers want the entire Amazon catalog, not a small, little piece of it. And Amazon prices are changing all the time, so when local database services provide sellers downloaded data on a memory card, that data is old the instant that the data download completes. Prices and Sales Ranks change constantly. A book that was good yesterday may not be good today. A dud book yesterday may be popular today because it was mentioned on Oprah; but if you have stale data, you would never know.

I was one of those sellers. I used a local database service, but the limitations became more and more evident. The need for a live service that displayed competitive FBA offers was desperately needed and that need was met with ScanPower. Just as FBA was a Game Changer in respect to selling online, ScanPower was a Game Changer in the world of mobile scanning.

The Current State of Scouting

Technology is constantly improving and companies are released better and faster tools to be used in this business. At the time of this writing, the third generation iPad is my device of choice. Here is an excerpt from a blog post that I wrote when it was released:

The new iPad HD was announced on March 7, 2012 and it included some great updates including a higher-resolution screen, faster processor, better camera, and 4G speeds. The Verizon version of the new iPad HD has an interesting twist that many people may have overlooked.

Many of you know that I have Sprint for my cell phone provider and chose to get an iPad 2 on Verizon specifically to use in places where I get no Sprint service. For this purpose, it works great; I have yet to go to a place where neither Sprint nor Verizon had service.

The new Verizon iPad HD takes this to a whole new level. According to BGR.com:

Even though the Verizon iPad supports LTE and CDMA, it's also a global device, and it supports all standard WCDMA and GSM bands as well. This means you can put an AT&T microSIM card in the Verizon iPad, and use AT&T's 3G network without a problem since all iPads are unlocked. Additionally, the Verizon iPad lets you connect up to five Wi-Fi devices to it so you can share that insanely fast LTE connection. http://www.bgr.com/2012/03/19/a-new-ipad-review/

Remember, iPad data is MONTH-TO-MONTH so there are no contracts to get into. You can get a Verizon iPad HD and turn on the data just for the months that you are scouting in an area where you need carrier-specific service.

Sprint not working? Use Verizon 4G. Verizon 4G not working? Use Verizon 3G. Verizon 3G not working? Use AT&T 3G. It would almost be a challenge to find somewhere where Sprint, Verizon, and AT&T had absolutely no service.

In addition to having backup services in the event of dead-zones, the Verizon iPad HD includes free mobile hotspot so you can share your data with up to five additional devices! You can go scouting with friends or family using iPod Touches, iPads, or Android tablets that don't need their own data plans since you are sharing the Verizon iPad HD's connection.

And you can have all of this backup and still just carry one cell phone and one iPad HD. It is an absolute WEAPON of a device for scouters.

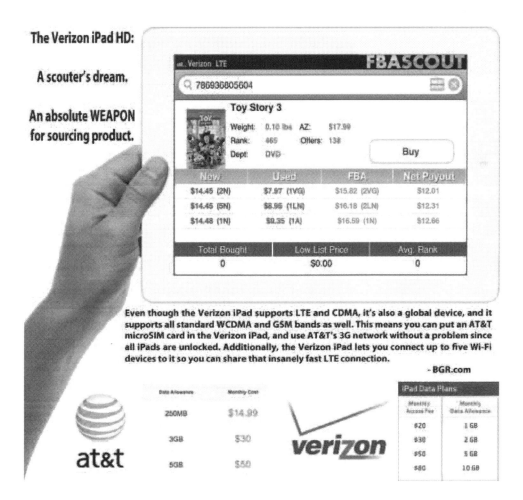

The Verizon iPad HD:

A scouter's dream.

An absolute WEAPON for sourcing product.

Even though the Verizon iPad supports LTE and CDMA, it's also a global device, and it supports all standard WCDMA and GSM bands as well. This means you can put an AT&T microSIM card in the Verizon iPad, and use AT&T's 3G network without a problem since all iPads are unlocked. Additionally, the Verizon iPad lets you connect up to five Wi-Fi devices to it so you can share that insanely fast LTE connection.

- BGR.com

Technology, hardware, and mobile data speeds will continue to improve making access to information faster and easier. Those who adapt will have an advantage over their competitors.

Free Alternatives

In addition to scouting apps like ScanPower, there are an increasing number of incredibly useful mobile apps that are absolutely free to download and use. While ScanPower is specifically designed for arbitrage and to quickly identifying resale opportunities, these other apps are designed for shopping. Even so, they provide a competitive pricing picture that can be useful in determining the online market value of an item to compare to the in-store or online price of that item.

These apps include:

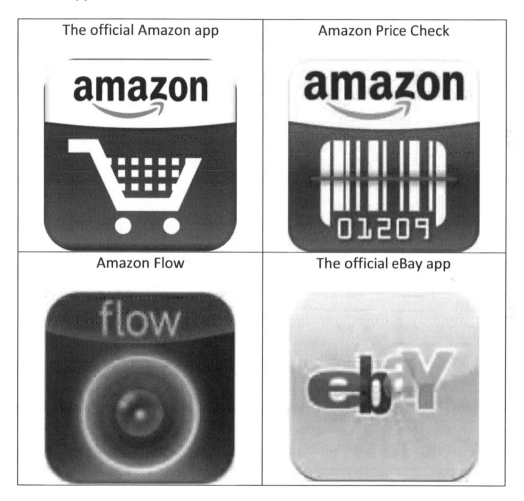

| The official Amazon app | Amazon Price Check |
| Amazon Flow | The official eBay app |

All of these apps are FREE and available for both iPhone/iPad and Android devices. Simply search in the Apple App Store or Google Play.

Chapter 8 – An Emerging Business Model

This all represents an emerging business model that has developed recently and it is the most powerful, profitable, low-risk, and completely scalable business model that may have ever existed. Running an FBA business using the strategies in this book for arbitrage is like nothing that has ever existed before. Without services like FBA to outsource the storage, picking, packing, shipping, and customer service, resellers will quickly run into the physical limitations of the real world that will basically put a cap on how large their business can grow. Without mobile pricing tools like ScanPower to source products and make increasingly risk-free buying decisions, resellers would have to rely on inferior methods for making buying decisions, which would lead to higher risks.

It is only very recently that all of the tools have been put in place to really create this new, emerging business model. It is truly an exciting time to be selling online. I've been selling online since 1999 and I've packed over 100 boxes a day, every day, day after day. That business model was profitable, but it's not ideal and it's not scalable. FBA opens the doors to anyone who wants to take advantage of the arbitrage opportunities all around them. They can start small and grow as big as they want to get. **Don't underestimate how powerful the scalability factor of FBA is.** It allows the little guy to start and compete with established sellers on day one and gives them the tools to grow as big as they want as fast as they want.

While ScanPower shows you the complete, current pricing picture for any item on Amazon, it is ultimately up to the user to make buying decisions. A good rule of thumb for doubling your money (100% margin) is the 1/3 – 1/3 – 1/3 rule if scouting for items to sell using FBA. Try to find items that are selling online for three times your cost. If you find a $10 item, you want it to be selling for $30. As rough estimates, you can consider your product cost to be $10, Amazon with all FBA fees will get $10, and your profit will be $10. Use this as a safety guide if you are just starting out.

While this 1/3 – 1/3 – 1/3 rule is easy to remember, it should not be a rule that you follow exclusively. We made up this guideline to help new sellers keep their margins high and protect themselves. We came up with using rough estimates of typical Amazon and FBA fees on items that we sold ourselves. Sometimes fees will be higher than 1/3 of the sales price and sometimes they will be lower. **It is vastly more important to learn the rules and fee structure of the Amazon marketplace and the FBA program than to rely on a guideline printed here.**

Some fees are fixed and will be the same regardless of the sales price on Amazon. Some fees will vary with the sales price such as the category-based commission. Because of these types of fees, the fees as a percentage of sales price will be **higher** on low-priced items than they will be on higher priced items.

Remember, the 1/3 – 1/3 – 1/3 rule is designed to help new sellers avoid risk by keeping their margins high.

100% margin is great, but making 50% on your money in a month is still pretty attractive (compare this to your local bank's rates). In the event that prices fall, a new seller will still have room to lower their price to remain competitive and while still turning a profit. If their margins were too low to begin with and prices fall, they will have a greater risk of losing money on their inventory.

Once you gain some experience on Amazon and become more familiar with the Amazon and FBA fee structures, you'll be more comfortable taking a lower margin than 100%. When you have confidence that an item will sell quickly and you'll realize your profit sooner rather than later, a lower margin can make a lot of sense.

You can also use the FBA Calculator to familiarize yourself with the Amazon fees:

https://sellercentral.amazon.com/gp/fbacalc/fba-calculator.html

Naturally, I encourage all resellers to shoot for the highest profit margins that they can find. Some sellers will be comfortable with margins under 100%. Even an item on which you are making 50% return on your money is a lot better than what you're getting at the bank, so keep it all in perspective.

Efficiency Is The Key

The key to this business model is efficiency. The technology and tools at the reseller's disposal are incredibly powerful. These tools didn't even exist just a few years ago. These tools allow anyone to make low-risk buying decisions. Without using the best tools, your risks increase and your business will not be running as efficiently as it could be.

Consider these two scenarios. One reseller drives to a store and writes down hundreds of UPCs and product descriptions by hand. Then they drive home and enter them one by one into Amazon.com. They go to many different pages of offers to see the complete competitive pricing picture for the item. They make notes about which items to buy then they drive back to the store. They go pick up the items on their shopping list and find out that two of the best products are now sold out. They check out with their items and drive back home to list them on Amazon.com.

Compare this to driving to a store and using a scouting app like ScanPower on your iPhone to evaluate any product instantly with one simple screen of pricing data. You don't miss a single deal. In fact, you find so many deals that you have to put some of the good deals back so that you can fit all of the great deals in your car. You upload your Buy List from your iPhone to your ScanPower account for listing while you are still standing in line to check out. You print your labels, you pack your boxes, and you're done.

It's easy to see how ScanPower pays for itself very quickly in saved time and improved efficiency.

Whether you started as a bookseller or not, consider how this business model emerged from the history of scouting you read about in Chapter 7.

Business Model Transition

Say you started as a bookseller and now you've now made the switch to FBA and life is good. More time to scout and you're finding good books to sell. You meet someone new and they ask what it is that you do and you tell them that you sell online. They ask what you sell, and you tell them books.

STOP: HERE IS THE CHANGE. HERE IS THE NEW BUSINESS MODEL.

Stop and ask yourself, "Why am I a bookseller again?" Go back to how it all started. Books: easy to find. Books: easy to scan. Books: easy to list. Books: easy to store. Books: easy to ship. But now you use FBA so the easy to store and easy to ship don't matter. As an FBA seller, you can sell items that may not be easy to store or easy to ship.

Let's look at the others: Easy to find, scan, and list.

Books are easy to find and can be found for prices lower than the market rate. This opens the door for profit to someone who has this information. Users could quickly see that information was power. Having good data was like putting on a special pair of glasses that would make profitable books turn green and non-profitable books turn red. You had super-vision while everyone else just saw a bunch of books.

HERE COMES THE SCOUTING CHANGE: you can now put these glasses on and find green products everywhere that you go. The last piece to this puzzle, the secret weapon, is ScanPower. ScanPower is the next evolution of mobile scouting. Like FBA, it is a true game changer. All limitations of other scouting services are overcome with ScanPower. Can you still scout for books? Of course! I still do because it's fun and profitable, but why box yourself in as a bookseller when you use ScanPower and FBA? Book sales only happen so often each month and if you live in a small town, they don't happen very often at all. Thrift stores only put out so many new books each day. With ScanPower, you have pricing data for every category on Amazon, not just books, so why are you just looking for books?

When people ask me what I do, I tell them I sell online. They ask what I sell and I tell them, "Profitable items." That's really the only criteria I have anymore. Why discriminate? Find a profitable item? Send it to FBA. The categories I generally sell the most in are Books, Media, Toys, and Home Improvement (power tools). This is just because I am most familiar with these categories. If there were more hours in a day I could branch out into as many categories as time would allow.

The thing to understand here is that there is a great change that is taking place. Many booksellers are right on the verge of seeing this incredible opportunity if they can take their 'book blinders' off. If you are using a scanner and using FBA, then you already have 95% of this 'machine' in place.

Step 1: Find profitable items
Step 2: Send to FBA
Step 3: Profit
Step 4: Repeat

Stop and ask yourself: why am I just doing this with books? The only real reason is that you have limited data from a book scouting service so you can't scan toys or power tools. Once you get ScanPower, the last piece of the puzzle is in place. 'Books: Easy to find' turns into 'Profitable Items: Easy to find'.

"But I make a lot of money on books! Why would I want to learn another category?"

I'm glad you asked. ☺

Think of it this way: you have your scout, you drive to a thrift store, poke around, scan some items, and find a book that will give you $20 profit. You buy that book. ONE BOOK.

Now, in that same amount of time that it took you to go out and find one book, you could have found one product from any number of retail stores that would yield that same $20 profit. But here's the kicker: you put 16 units in your cart. 16 times more profit for the same amount of work. Live in a big city, go to another store and buy the same item again. If you sell out on Amazon, just go buy more and replenish your stock.

How is this possible? It's actually very easy; the markets are terribly inefficient! Do you think Wal-Mart always has the lowest price? Nope. How about Costco? No way items are cheaper on Amazon than from Costco, right? Wrong. The market is inefficient and it goes both ways. A $10 item on the shelf at Wal-Mart can be selling for $40 on Amazon. A $10 item on Amazon can be selling for $40 at Wal-Mart. ScanPower is like putting on special glasses when you walk into a store that tells you any pricing inefficiencies between Amazon and that store. Think of green and red dollar signs floating over each item. Some of them are bigger than others. Now go find the biggest green ones.

In addition, you'll know if an item is not on Amazon at all. The opportunities that this represents are covered in more detail in Bonus #2 at the end of this book.

On top of this, you can scout at retail stores all day and all night! Many stores open 24/7. You are not limited by thrift store hours or library sale schedules. Even if you have young kids at home all day, you can stay up late and make that extra income in the early morning hours. There is no other business in which you can set your own hours like an FBA business. You choose if you want to schedule your month around library sales, or scout at your leisure for retail products.

Here are the exact steps to take if you are brand new to buying products to sell online.

1. You need to find products to sell.

While you don't need a subscription scouting service like ScanPower to start, it will quickly become apparent as to how valuable they are in terms of efficiency. You could go to a store and write down UPCs by hand, then go home and look them all up and make some calculations, and then decide which items to sell online, and then go back to the store and purchase the items. Not a very efficient process, but you get the idea.

So to use ScanPower you do need an iPhone, iPad or an Android phone or tablet. All major US cell phone companies carry a wide variety of Android devices. You also need a data connection such as Wi-Fi, 3G, or 4G.

When to Get The Scanfob® 2002

You can start on the cheap by using the camera to capture barcodes using a barcode-scanning app like RedLaser on iPhone or ZXing on Android. This requires you to hold the camera above the UPC in order to capture the barcode. This isn't hard, but it is not the most efficient solution. The Scanfob® 2002 is a data entry device and it dramatically increases the speed at which you can enter data into ScanPower. The Scanfob® 2002 is a Bluetooth scanner, meaning that it connects wirelessly to your phone over Bluetooth technology. Once connected, the Scanfob® 2002 sends the UPC to your phone instantly. You can reach up high and shoot the Scanfob® 2002 scanner at barcodes on items on the overhead shelves and get the pricing data on your phone. Compare this to having to get the item down from the overhead shelves and having to position your phone over the barcode for each and every item for which you are checking prices. It can even capture UPCs through glass display cases.

The right equipment will pay for itself very quickly in the time saved. When you save time in one area of your business, you have more time to spend in other areas. When you have more time, you can scan more items. Scanning more items means that you'll find more profitable items.

The Scanfob® 2002 is about $300 and is available from http://www.serialio.com. There is a coupon code on the ScanPower website that gives ScanPower users a discounted price. I strongly recommend adding the Scanfob® 2002 to your ScanPower setup.

2. Now that you have items to sell, you need to get them listed

This book is all about using FBA for order fulfillment on Amazon but you don't necessarily have to use FBA. Now that you have items to sell, you can list them on Amazon and ship them yourself. To sell using FBA, you follow the listing process outlined on Amazon.com. When you are ready to increase your efficiency, you can start to use ScanPower.

ScanPower is our listing program that will dramatically increase the speed at which you can list, price, and label your FBA inventory. Save time here, and you'll have more time for the other, more profitable parts of your business such as sourcing additional products.

3. Now that you have items listed for sale, you need to keep them priced competitively

This is where repricing programs come in. ScanPower includes a repricer but it's really not needed until your inventory gets to a level that makes it difficult to reprice manually. Don't worry about learning to use a repricer if you don't have anything listed for sale online!

Repricing programs not only help you keep your items priced competitively, they also helps you leverage your status as an FBA seller and maximize the margins on your items. They should be saving you time be helping you adjust your prices quickly AND accurately to stay competitive but still maintain your margins.

That's pretty much the evolution of scouting and how it has evolved into the current business model that it is today. It is hard to describe all of the ways that you can use FBA in your business, but throughout this book, I will do my best.

Chapter 9 – From Toys to Toiletries

I think you are starting to get the idea here that this emerging business model is wide open. There are really no limits as to what you can sell online through FBA (some categories are restricted, so be sure to read the Amazon rules covered in Chapter 12).

You can choose to be a 100% widget seller who pays no attention to what is actually in the boxes that they sell. You can just scan to your heart's content, run the numbers, and send the profitable stuff to FBA. Or you can decide to focus on certain categories.

There are advantages and disadvantages to both types of models. When you consider yourself a widget seller, you don't really have any limits as to where you scout or what you scout for. But if you don't increase your knowledge in any specific area, then you may be leaving a lot of opportunities behind. Scouting in and learning a specific category such as the Health & Personal Care category (formerly Health and Beauty Accessories) can be very rewarding because you learn what to look for. When you have had success with a product line, you can more easily identify opportunities when you see them based on your experience. Your previous experience gives you an advantage over another seller who's only using price and margin to make buying decisions. Your experience can help you take advantage of seasonal swings in supply and demand as well as specific local retailer secrets that can give you a huge advantage.

You also learn what makes a product a good fit for FBA and in turn you are able to more quickly evaluate other potentially good items with more speed and efficiency.

Most FBA sellers will probably end up selling a blend of inventory that includes some pretty random, but profitable items alongside their staple products with which they are more familiar. Personally, I am a widget seller when it comes to books and media. When it comes to power tools and toys, I pay more attention to factors such as the brand, exclusivity, margin, competition, and other factors that affect the item's resale value.

Items can be very lucrative in the Health & Personal Care category (formerly Health & Beauty Accessories). Not only can you find items at retail stores at prices that are much lower than the Amazon.com marketplace prices, but there are also added dynamics at play in this category.

Some people fall in love with a certain brand of shampoo, their favorite eyeliner, or a specific scent of hand lotion. People who put a high personal preference on items such as these will go to greater lengths than other buyers in order to get the specific product that they want. **Some will be willing to pay a little more, and some will be willing to pay A LOT MORE.** This happens all the time when a manufacturer discontinues certain products that some buyers have a strong, personal connection with. If you are able to identify these types of items, you can bring this limited supply to the demand and keep the profit in between. The buyers of these types of products will thank you that they are able to acquire the limited supply from your part of the country even though they live on the other side of the country. If they didn't value the item that you're selling for your selling price, then they would not have purchased the item.

These same dynamics do exist in other categories so be on the lookout for items that have these same types of characteristics.

Another category in particular that I want to share information with you about is the Toys & Games category. This is one of the easiest and most profitable categories in which to buy and sell using ScanPower and FBA. I want to explain WHY Toys & Games is such a great category and how you can have great success in this category as well.

There are many reasons why toys are so profitable. Toys are heavily marketed to kids and popular toys can be in high demand. High demand can mean high prices, especially if supply is low. When demand outweighs supply, prices rise. They don't rise at the retail level because retail stores have agreements in place with the manufacturers. But on the secondary market, price is set by the forces of supply and demand.

Don't think that toys only sell at Christmas time. Sure, this category sees a huge boost at Christmas time, but kids have birthdays all year long. And don't think that it's only Christmas and birthdays when kids get presents. There are occasions throughout the year. These days kids even by their own toys with their own money.

Toys are also pretty universal in terms of UPCs. Amazon has sold a lot of toys over the years and will already have product pages for most every toy that you can scan. Remember, if you scan a toy and it has no match on Amazon, then you may have just found another opportunity to create a new product page and be the only seller and setting your own price.

Toys are different in the sense that the demand for them can be very specific. It's not like power tools where someone will say to their wife that they would like a new drill for Father's Day and pretty much any drill will do. There will be a demand for a Super Duper Talking Optimus Prime with Bonus Bumblebee Walkie-Talkie Playset. This is a specific demand, not a 'please buy me an Optimus Prime for my birthday' type demand.

Toys come and go at the retail level. This means that items get clearanced and prices drop. This is how you can often buy toys for well below the original MSRP. Just because the demand for these toys is not walking into your local Toys R Us, it doesn't mean that the demand is not still out there looking for these toys. Some of that demand is looking on Amazon, and you can bring that supply to the marketplace and enjoy the profit of the difference in price.

Retail Exclusives

Some toys are exclusive to certain retailers. This can create an online demand at a premium price over the local retail price. Why? Because some buyers do not live near each and every retailer. The only way that someone can get an exclusive item is to buy it from someone who lives near the exclusive store and is willing to offer it for sale online. Couldn't they just purchase the item from the retailer's website? Not always. Later in Chapter 19 I'll explain the difference between local retail stores and their online counterparts and why their inventories and even product selection do not always match up.

A reseller is only going to go to this trouble of buying and listing an item if they are able to turn a profit. Two examples of retailers who often have exclusive toys are Toys R Us and Target. They are easy to spot because they have big stickers on the packages that say 'Toys R Us Exclusive' or 'Only At Target'. Stores like to have exclusive products because it can be a draw to get customers into their stores for products that are not available elsewhere. They also do not have to worry about price matching other retailers because no other retailer will have the exact same product.

Consider this as well; toys are collectible. There are collectors out there that want to collect every single Lego set ever made. Maybe they are collecting every single Transformer toy ever. If they want them all and they don't live near every retailer that offers any version of an exclusive, then they will have to find and buy the items online. Like we mentioned before, price set by supply and demand. There may also be collectors who take an interest in a product line long after the toy series was actually current and available on toy shelves. If they want to collect the toys and they are not currently available at all retail stores, then they will have to buy on the secondary market.

Getting Lucky? Or Being Smart?

Not all Toys R Us stores are going to carry the exact same items. Some stores will turn over their inventory much faster than other stores and some will be very slow moving. A toy may become popular and sell out at most stores but you can get lucky and find them still sitting on the shelf at other stores. This may be because it's a store that people normally do not associate with toys. I bought Nintendo Wii controllers from Sears the year that the Wii was released. Everything Wii was sold out everywhere, or so people thought. Where do you go to buy video games? Toys R Us? Target? Wal-Mart? Best Buy? Sure, but Sears? It was not the first place that people think of so people didn't go there. I did and sold a ton of $40 Nintendo Wii controllers for over $100 each . ☺

Because some stores don't sell the same items at the same rates as other stores, some stores will have products still on the shelves that other stores sold out of a long time ago. Maybe this toy was not even good for resale at the time it was released but has enjoyed some kind of recent surge in popularity (demand). These toys may be nowhere to be found but if you keep your eyes open, you can get lucky and find them sitting lonely on a shelf somewhere, still waiting for a buyer.

Stores may also only appear to be sold out. If there are no products on the shelf, look in the overheads. Ask the store employees to check the computer inventory system. Maybe they have more in the back. Maybe they know when more are due to arrive at the store. Maybe they can check the inventory levels at another store for you.

When Toys Are HOT

Every year there are tons of new toys that are marketed to kids. Some of these toys end up being THE TOY. This is the toy that every kid has to have. The marketing done by the toy companies created strong demand and when this demand outweighs the supply, prices rise and a strong secondary market emerges. This happens all the time. This is simple economics being played out in real life. It happens a lot around Christmas time, but this phenomenon happens to different toys all year long. Learning the toy market will help you capitalize on this imbalance in supply and demand and leave you with the profit.

There is a bonus chapter at the end of this book called The Pixar Effect (Bonus #5) that goes into greater details about the different dynamics affecting today's retail toys. Supply and demand, even when very small, can now still find each other through the Internet. This is affecting the price of retail toys long after they are pulled from the retail store shelves to make room for the latest and greatest toys.

Remember the chapter about Understanding the Amazon Buyer? That applies here as well. Parents want to buy online and some of those parents want to buy from Amazon.com as their online seller of choice. Price is a factor in the purchasing decision, but it is not always the deciding factor.

Chapter 10 – THE TIME TO ACT IS NOW!

The pieces that make arbitrage work on this scale have never before been available in the way that they are today. Without FBA, this type of business would only appeal to entrepreneurs who are willing to fill up their garages with products and commit to processing orders on a daily basis. Without ScanPower, making the best buying decisions would be increasingly risky. Without a guide like *Arbitrage For Fun & Profit* and the online FBA support communities that have developed (see Additional Resources at the end of this book), you'd be on your own to make mistakes and try to figure this all out for yourself. This guide will allow you to avoid the learning curve of this business and allow you to start making profits from day one. Now is the perfect time to get in on this emerging business model.

You may be asking yourself, "If other people are already doing arbitrage, is there still money to be made? Or is it too late?" It's a good question. Always remember, this is a business model of abundance and not one of scarcity. Later in this book under Bonus #3, I'll explain why it's simply not possible for any one person or company to take over all of the arbitrage opportunities that exist out there today.

This is a cutting-edge business and you'll be using some very high-tech products. It can be a little overwhelming at first, but if you have questions, there are many places online where you can get help. There is an Additional Resources section at the end of this book with tons of resources and links to online communities that are happy to help new sellers.

The important thing to do is to act; you have to get started. There are deals out there just waiting to be discovered. Consider this like a franchise opportunity but where the cost of entry is practically zero. If you already have an iPhone or Android device, you can download the ScanPower trial and get 250 free scans today. Go to a store like Big Lots or Toys R Us and see if what is written in this book is true or not. Then the only thing stopping you from starting your own arbitrage business is putting the items in your cart, checking out, and listing them for sale online.

This type of business will continue to grow and get bigger and better over time. Amazon is moving in the right direction and they are giving third party sellers incredibly powerful tools to help them succeed that were not imaginable just a few short years ago. Amazon is growing at a fantastic pace with too many opportunities to count. If you share this vision and want to participate in this growth, I encourage you to get in now and enjoy the ride.

The Fourth Quarter

The fourth quarter, sometimes called Q4, is the common term for the last three months of the year. It includes the Christmas shopping season, which will see a huge surge in retail sales (both in store and online). Don't let the fourth quarter sneak up on you! Be prepared to take advantage of the huge opportunities that the fourth quarter brings every year.

The following pages contain our actual Amazon payouts from Q4 2009 and Q4 2010. You'll see an increase leading up to December 25th and then you'll see a sales decline. This happens every year as the Q4 spike in sales comes back down to normal levels.

You'll also see the returns increase. This will happen to you after Christmas as well, so don't be alarmed. It just comes with the territory of selling in any kind of serious volume. Buyers purchased many of these items for gifts, and some are returned. Many of your returns will go straight back into sellable inventory. **Remember, you can only get a lot of returns if you sell a lot of stuff!**

Here you can see the nice surge in sales that we received in 2009. Note the dates. Sales always taper off right after Christmas.

November 9, 2009 – November 23, 2009

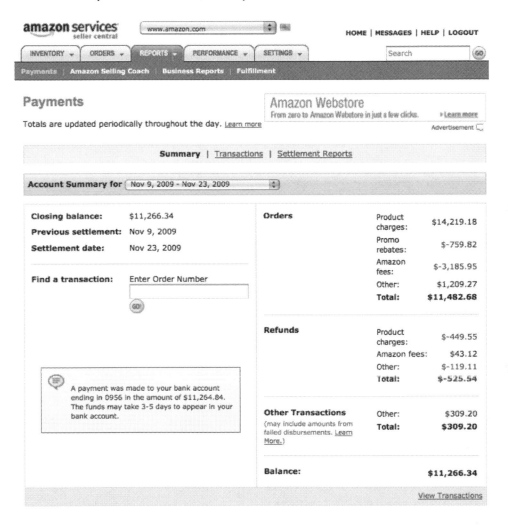

November 23, 2009 – December 7, 2009

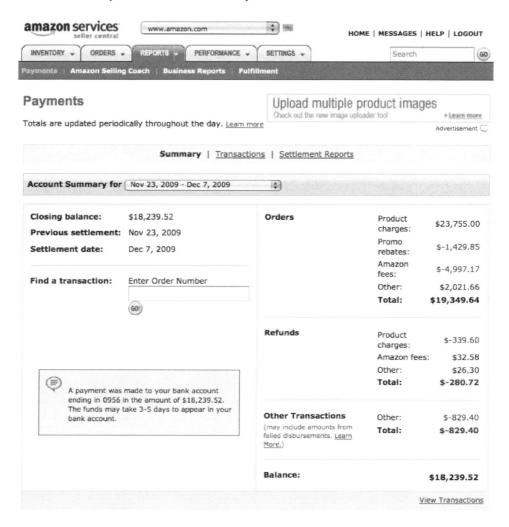

December 7, 2009 – December 21, 2009

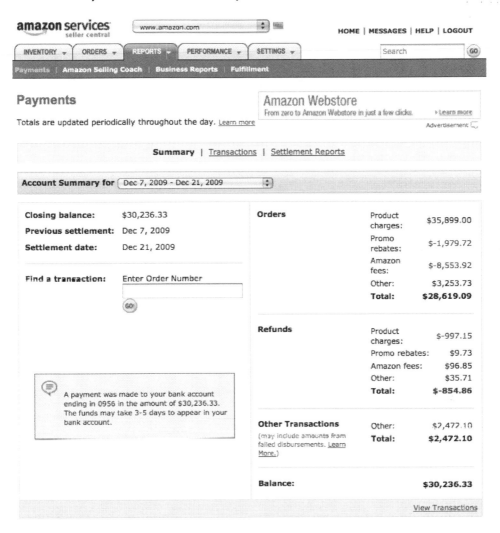

December 21, 2009 – January 4, 2010

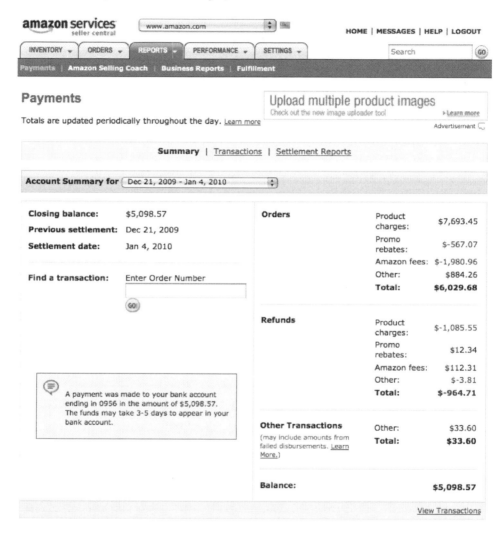

You'll see the sales already tapering off as this payout period only had a few days of sales prior to December 25th.

January 4, 2010 – January 18, 2010

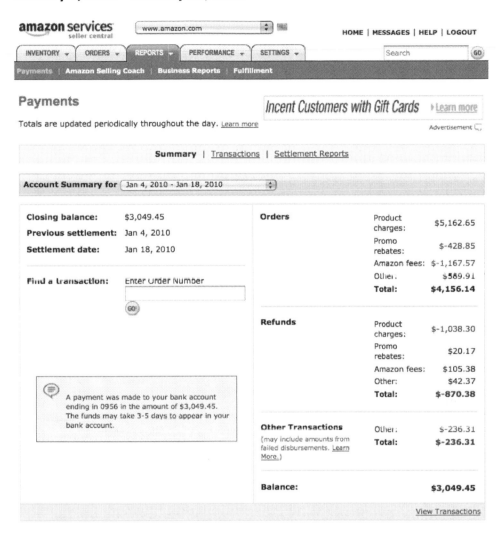

Sales continue to taper off, as buyers are not buying at the same level as before Christmas.

Here you can see a nice surge in sales that we received in 2010. Note the dates. Sales always taper off right after Christmas.

November 8, 2010 – November 22, 2010

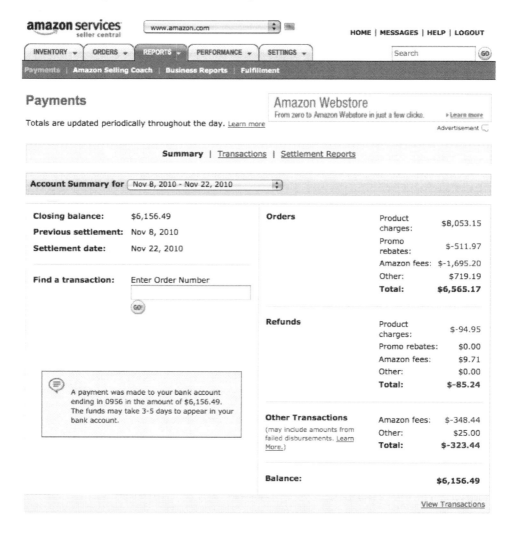

November 22, 2010 – December 6, 2010

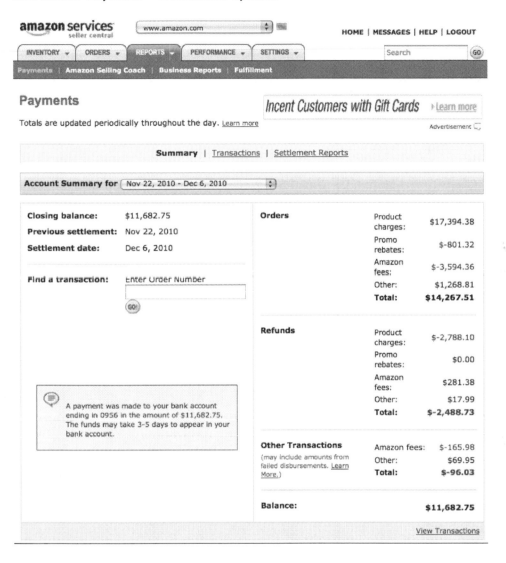

December 6, 2010 – December 20, 2010.

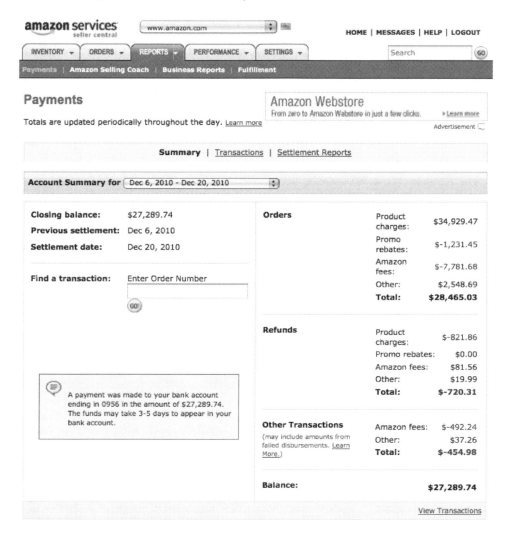

December 20, 2010 – January 3, 2011

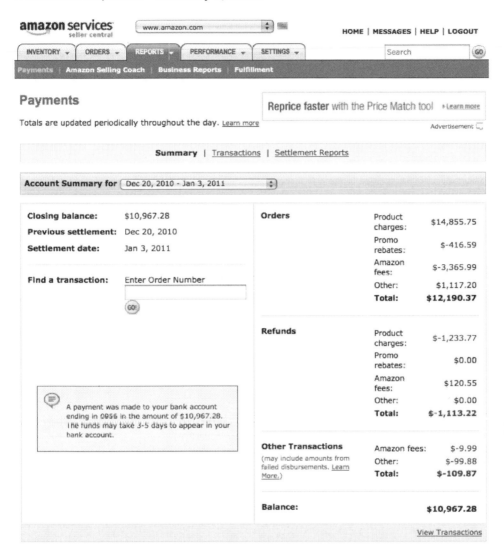

Sales stayed stronger this year than last year, but still showed a sharp decline from pre-December 25th levels.

January 3, 2011 – January 17, 2011

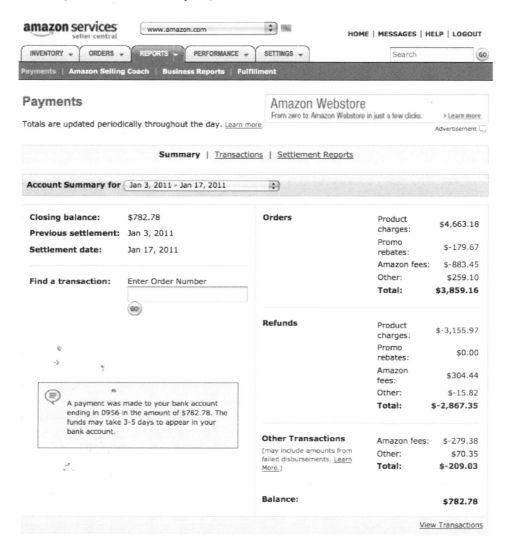

Whoa! Big decline in sales post Q4 and more returns. No surprises here. It happens every year.

You can see for yourself the kinds of numbers that are possible with this business. Don't let another Q4 pass you by without getting in on the action!

IMPORTANT: Don't psych yourself out of this opportunity. Are there other resellers out there doing arbitrage right now? You bet there are; they are out there and they are making money every day. But as I explain in detail in Bonus #3 at the end of this book, no one can do all of the deals out there. When you are buying and selling items from retail stores or hitting up book sales and thrift stores, do not talk yourself out of being disciplined and evaluating the products for yourself. Just because someone else has scanned an item and deemed it not a good match for their individual business model, it doesn't necessarily mean that the item is not a good match for your business model.

I've seen it so many times and I've even felt that feeling myself. If I get to a book sale late and I see other scanners, I start to think that maybe I should just pack it in. All of the good books are probably gone already, right? Or I see someone walking out of Toys R Us with a ton of stuff and wonder if maybe they are a reseller like me. They probably already got all of the good stuff already, right? **WRONG; always wrong.** I make myself stay and it always pays off. I've included tons of information in this book as to why this mentality of scarcity is incorrect later in this book in Bonus #7: Your Lazy Competition.

Get your head in the game and remember that this is fun and rewarding work, but it is work nonetheless. Those who put in the work will reap the rewards. Will this be you? Are you willing to test if what is written in this book is true or not?

Chapter 11 – Anyone Can Do This

I truly believe that anyone can do this business. All it takes is a little motivation and some consistency and you will start to see the opportunities that are all around you. All you have to do is take the first step to making it happen. I have personally trained and mentored many FBA sellers and I truly enjoy doing so. It is rewarding to know that you are really helping someone make that extra income that they need. An FBA business is fairly unique in the sense that you really can work when you want to work and stop working anytime. There are really no commitments. Like I mentioned earlier in this book, this type of business simply did not exist in this form just a few short years ago.

While anyone can do this, this is not a get-rich-quick type of business. This business is work and it can be very rewarding work, especially financially, but you do have to learn this business. Just doing what someone tells you to do or buy what someone tells to you to buy won't do you any good in the long term. I want to see you succeed long term with this business but that involves you making the decision to hit the streets and get yourself familiar with all aspects of this business. Don't be afraid to make mistakes; I know I've made a ton of them! The good thing about making mistakes? You learn from them and you can take steps to not make them again.

So can anyone do this business? Absolutely! But the ones who commit, work, and learn this business through and through will be the ones with long term success. Will this be you?

I've included three testimonials from three different people that I have worked with over the past few years. They all include a link to their Amazon stores as well as their email addresses. I asked them if this was OK and they all said, "Of course!" I get just as skeptical as you probably do when you see all the glowing reviews on a website, they are all fairly vague, and they are all from important sounding people like John H.,

Amazon seller, or Jane Q., Amazon seller. Who is this Jane Q.? How do I know she is not just some made up person? What if I want to ask her a question about her testimonial? Or see their Amazon store? These testimonials are the real deal from real people and you are welcome to contact them with questions.

In the interest of full disclosure, I will say upfront that one is going to be totally biased because it's from my mom, but her story is an inspiring one. She is our number one scanner in terms of number of products scanned. She can claim this title because she is CONSISTENT. She goes out scanning on a schedule and sticks to it. She almost always finds something, but there are times where she comes home empty handed and that's OK. She was able to retire early and travel often thanks to her FBA business.

Having to teach this business to my mom was actually a huge blessing in disguise. This forced us to make sure the program was 'Grandma-compatible'. If it wasn't easy for her to use, then it wasn't easy enough for other people to use. You could call her the ultimate Grandma beta tester!

Anyone Can Do This

Nancy Green

Let me introduce myself - I'm 'Anybody', also known as the FBA Grandma, and I can do it. I will also disclose that Chris is my son and undoubtedly that gave me a big advantage when I was starting out on this adventure. A little background about myself: I've been a treasure hunter most of my life, from furnishing my college apartment, to stocking my booth at Antique Malls, and even filling out my wardrobe. Several years ago when I was still working full time, I was selling some of my 'found treasures' on eBay. While it was worthwhile financially I must admit that I did not enjoy the process of listing the items, taking pictures, monitoring the emails, and then packing, labeling and shipping the treasures that I sold.

While in college, Chris was also selling on eBay and then he continued to use eBay as a source of income after graduation. As the volume of his sales grew to be too much to easily ship daily, he discovered FBA. What a perfect solution! He then became interested in selling books as he researched and realized the profits that could be made. Knowing that I love to treasure hunt in thrift stores and garage sales, he explained the whole process to me. We started out with scanners that we uploaded data into, then set parameters and started scanning books and listening for the bell to ring. Then we had to list, label and pack the books. Well that was okay (I was making money), but my son has always liked to do things the most efficient way possible. The fact that the data wasn't current or complete, and the time consuming process of listing and shipping really bothered him. I'll let him tell you that part of the story...

So - when he first came out with ScanPower I guess I was one of the first to use it. It's just so easy. I actually have my scanner attached to the back of my phone with Velcro and it goes everywhere with me. I use the EVO on Sprint and I can assure you that I only carry a phone like this because Chris bought it for me (and now for ScanPower).

While I was working, I would head out to a thrift store or two on my lunch hour. I was really lucky because there were several close to the office. Now, you have to remember that this is a treasure hunt, so some days I might only find a couple of books that I felt would be worthwhile buying to resell, but then the next day there would be a whole box of good books. I try to buy most of my books for a dollar or less with a minimum selling price of $8.00, but I will spend up to $3.00 when I see that the value is $11.00 or more. I think everyone will set his or her own parameters as they become familiar with all the information on the screen. I used to not see that Amazon was selling the book, and often for less than anyone else. I only did that a few times! I also check to see how may books are at the lowest price because, sometimes once two or three have been sold you'll see that the market price is now worthwhile. All week long I would fill up my trunk and then one night I would unload them and stack them by size on my worktable. (It just makes it so much easier to pack the boxes.)

ScanPower just makes it so easy and efficient to list, price, and label my items. I find that it usually takes me about an hour to complete a box. A portion of that time is removing labels, cleaning any marks, and checking for highlights or underlining on the pages. I usually ship two to three boxes every week.

After I retired I found that I was changing my 'booking' schedules because I could now take advantage of certain sale days at the various stores. Tuesdays are Senior's Day so I have a regular route to take advantage of the 25 - 30% discounts. I can also now go to stores that are further away. I just pick a community that is close, Google for "thrift stores" and then decide if it looks worthwhile to make a trip. I always print out the map and then make notes about the shops before and after I've been there. I keep all these sheets in a binder in the car. Usually one day a week I will head out of town, and it's always an adventure.

Now the best parts - finding books for $.49 to $1.00 that scan for $48.00 or $63.00 or even $89.00 or more! And even better - seeing that they sold and my Amazon payments account is growing. The fact that every two weeks a deposit appears in my bank account has allowed me to travel. Even when I've been away and haven't sent in books, something always sells.

I attended the SCOE 2011 convention this summer and was amazed at how huge the Amazon marketplace really is. With the FBA program the sky really is the limit. Being able to scan the whole catalog is amazing. Sometimes I wish I were 30 years younger because it is a very exciting time to be in ecommerce. However, my empire building days are over and I think I'll stick to my books (and maybe a few toys) where I have a comfort level of what works for the amount of time I want to spend with generous returns for my effort.

Yes, anyone can do it and with the educational materials and customer support that FBAPower offers you should seriously think about trying it yourself. It's fun to be on your own schedule, but it's also easy to scan for a couple of hours while you have a full time job.

I ran my numbers for 2010 for my accountant and came out with some pretty round numbers.

Total spent on inventory (mostly books): ~$8,000

Total Amazon payouts (not sales, payouts to my bank): ~$32,000

So ~$24,000 profit. I like to think of it as turning $1 into $4 about eight thousand times in a year.

This doesn't even account for all the books that are still at FBA that had not sold prior to December 31, 2010.

So, not a million dollars, but enough to make me feel confident enough to retire a little early.

Nancy Green, Irving, TX

http://www.amazon.com/shops/smoxie

nancyjgreen@gmail.com

I met Phyllis Anderson when I was selling scanner hardware (pre-ScanPower days) on eBay with a mentoring package. My favorite story about Phyllis (and I tell it all the time) is how she called me one day and had a new problem; she was making too much money to stay on Social Security! I told her that this is a great problem to have! My advice was to go find a good CPA who can help. She has managed to successfully branch out from just selling books and now sells practically anything that is profitable. She has also since trained several family members who are now also running successful FBA businesses. Here is her story:

Anyone Can Do This

By Phyllis Anderson

I am 64 years in age and sort of in the sandwich generation. I retired two years ago and became the caregiver for my mother. My youngest child (age 30) also needed some assistance in completing his education and raising his children. It wasn't long after I retired that I realized Social Security and my pension combined only allowed minimal survival. So to earn extra income I began throwing stuff on eBay and trying to earn extra cash by selling family heirlooms and estate sale items. I ran out of those pretty quickly and needed to do something that would create a steadier part-time stream of income. However, I could not re-enter the workplace due to my mother's health. I needed a way to make money that would fit my lifestyle.

While surfing eBay late one night I noticed Chris Green's eBay listing. It was for a book scanner, but his auction went on to say that he would personally train anyone purchasing one of the scanners on how to make money using Amazon's FBA program. He added that it was easy; Amazon shipped all of your products for you and that eliminated the part that was so time consuming with other online sales (the packing, shipping, and ongoing customer service). I was skeptical, but desperate. He included his phone number in the auction so I contacted Chris to find out more. He promised that my online purchase of a scanner from him would guarantee me the opportunity to learn FBA and that all questions would be welcome. He has more than lived up to his promise.

I purchased my scanner in March 2010 from Chris and began scanning barcodes and ISBNs at estate sales, library book sales, flea markets, and just about every retail store that I frequented. I have had lots of questions along the way and Chris has always answered them in a very positive upbeat way. I can't say enough about his honesty and integrity. Had I not been able to rely on his knowledge and expertise, it is quite likely that I never would have tried, or succeeded, with FBA.

With Chris's guidance, I was successful enough in my first year of FBA to have to worry about exceeding my Social Security earnings ceiling! Wow! Earning too much money to stay on Social Security was a problem I hadn't figured on! Believe me, following Chris's FBA program will make you successful whether you want a part-time or full-time income. When he introduced ScanPower last fall I ditched my old scanner and purchased an Android phone and the Scanfob® 2002. Now I do online sales of everything that I can find including books, grocery items, health and beauty products, and toys. It has opened up a whole new world of online selling for me.

There are so many things about this program that I love:

- Knowing that Chris and the other staff at ScanPower are there to support you whenever needed
- Allowing me the flexibility to work when and where I want (FBA online sales really do allow you to earn money while you sleep)
- Leaving the customer service and shipping to Amazon (providing me the time I need to scout for more products for resale)
- Best thing of all? Anyone can do this!

Phyllis Anderson, Des Moines, IA

http://www.amazon.com/shops/littlephilly

phphuber@hotmail.com

Phyllis Andersen UPDATE!

Phyllis has created her own website and written a book detailing her experiences on Amazon and with the FBA program. She shares her unique perspectives with the goal of helping others who are in her same situation. She's not trying to make a million dollars and she wants to have the flexibility to work when she wants to and care for aging family members as needed.

Here website is here: http://www.thriftyandsixty.com/

And her book is available here:

Thrifty & Sixty: The Simple and Easy Guide to Selling Online

http://www.amazon.com/dp/1479116882/

I also met Cynthia Stine through our eBay listing. She was completely new to selling on Amazon and this whole scanning books business. She had never heard of FBA. At the time, we were in Massachusetts and Cynthia said that she lived in Dallas/Fort Worth. We would be returning to Dallas/Fort Worth in a few months so we planned to meet up in order to get all of her questions answered. She was a quick and eager learner and she has really run with the FBA program. She came with me on a trip to Big Lots to see first-hand how to scout for items to resell. It can be such a huge help to see someone really doing this business. When you see someone scan an item, then put all forty-two of them in their cart with confidence, you see that finding good deals on items to sell online really are just as easy as people say that they are. It can give you the confidence to make that first big purchase. Here is her story:

Anyone Can Do This

By Cynthia Stine

How I pay for my son's private school…

My life changed dramatically in 2010. My husband and I adopted our teenage son, Eric. The clients for my consulting business went away – some of them owing me large sums of money – or greatly reduced their retainers, and we were overwhelmed with new expenses for our special needs son. I wanted to take advantage of my business slow-down to spend as much time as possible with him, but I also needed to bring in enough extra money to pay for his private school and other monthly expenses – about $1500 to $2000 more a month.

Selling on eBay bewildered me and it was so time-consuming just to get something photographed and listed. Amazon also seemed complicated and time-consuming until I discovered Amazon's FBA program through an online e-book. Once I grasped that I could sell penny books for $4 (or $5 or $7!), I never looked back.

Since I needed a streamlined operation where I could be productive on only a few hours a week, I signed up for ScanPower. It was well worth the money compared to the incredibly confusing spreadsheet that Amazon wanted me to fill out and upload. When ScanPower became available, I turned in my PDA scanner and doubled my income in a month thanks to real-time intelligence on Amazon listings and better thinking about my business.

The week I got my Scanfob® 2002 scanner, I met with Chris Green and went on a Big Lots shopping trip with him. In one afternoon, my business was turbo-charged. I realized that I was no longer an online bookseller, but an Amazon seller. I bought toys, baby items, Nintendo Wii accessories, calendars – anything with a barcode was now part of my business. For the first time I exceeded $2,000 a month from my Amazon business.

Besides understanding that I could sell in nearly every category, I also learned from Chris that I could often sell for MORE than a merchant seller could because my customer was really the Amazon Prime buyer and they are an impatient breed who will pay more to get it NOW. I signed up for Prime myself so I could understand – and I understand all too well now. Having to wait three to five days for something now seems like agony.

In addition, I learned that just because I would never pay high prices for some of these items (like a plastic baby spoon or a pacifier), it doesn't mean that someone else wouldn't. There are people who don't like to shop, people who live far away from shops, people who are very busy and people who are willing to pay extra for the convenience and speed. This is the nature of arbitrage and while I was initially doubtful of some of the things Chris told me that afternoon, I've learned he is right and I've adjusted my thinking.

For example, I have one product that I sell where I am the ONLY seller – not just the only FBA seller. As an experiment, I keep raising the price every time I send in new inventory. I can't believe how much people are willing to pay for this piece of plastic foam. I net about $30 on every sale. There are similar products on Amazon that are cheaper and that surely come up when my customers search, but they want this one. I will be so sad when I can't find any more because I sell about one a day when I have stock.

Before I had ScanPower, I would sometimes make mistakes because until I got home and listed the item, I could not see how many FBA sellers there were and their prices for the item. Now I always know ahead of time and can avoid the items with too many FBA sellers.

Chris taught me to scan everything and I take my scanner with me everywhere. One day at the Blockbuster Video, I noticed they were clearing out some weird items like "As Seen on TV!" sweepers, wall stickers for kids' rooms, Silly Bandz, Star Wars toys, and a bunch of other stuff that shouldn't have been there in the first place. They were on sale 75% to 90% off and I nearly squealed when I saw the rankings and prices on Amazon. I like to get at least a 3X return on an item I buy for resale. In this case, I was getting as much as 25X.

A friend introduced me to a thrift store that sells paperback books for 10 cents and hardbacks for 20 cents on Saturdays. They also sell video games for 15 cents and VHS tapes for 25 cents. I've taken $20 and turned it into hundreds of dollars on those Saturdays. We've never seen another scanner there. While we sell many of the books for $5-$7, we've found some for $40 and up that have really made us happy. At this same hole-in-the-wall store, we've found brand new medical supplies, adult diapers and other brand new items on which we've made huge profits. I bought a couple of cans of medical drink powder for $3 that sold for $50 online. You just never know what you will find if you look – and have the means to capitalize on it.

With FBA, I pay very little for warehousing. My last payment was $44 for over 2000 items. I used to have a 10'X10' storage unit for my primary business that cost me $80 a month. It still amazes me that I am able to leverage all the shipping, warehouse, logistics, and sales tools of the largest online retailer on earth for myself. I have a presence on Amazon and it costs me so little.

I live in one of the largest metropolitan areas in the country and yet I rarely see another scanner except at library book sales (and most of them are clearly not FBA and certainly not using ScanPower). When I go to a book sale full of scanners, I am still usually by myself wondering why the other people are wasting their time on penny books instead of grabbing the DVDs, textbooks and other non-fiction books that will sell for high-dollar amounts.

I went to Half-Price Books' 20% off sale over Labor Day and bought around $1000 worth of textbooks and Spanish language programs that I listed for over $5000. Selling through Amazon's FBA program is like turning straw into gold.

If you can't tell, I love my Amazon FBA business. The thrill of finding something with that right mix of rank and price is hard to describe – getting the check two weeks later is even better. I couldn't do it without my tools. I'm a huge fan of ScanPower because they give me competitive information that makes me a much more productive and profitable seller. I'm a small fry compared to others and only have about 30 hours a month I can put in (many of them after Eric's bedtime), but I'm very happy with the results. By leveraging the smarts and tools of ScanPower and Amazon's FBA program, I can achieve my personal and financial goals in a short amount of time each month.

Cynthia Stine, Dallas, TX

http://amzn.to/mypromotebooks

cynthia@promotesuccesspr.com

Cynthia Stine UPDATE!

Cynthia was already running a successful arbitrage business using FBA, but then she decided to really take things to the next level. She started her own website and wrote a book about how she makes thousands of dollars every month in just ten hours a week!

She admittedly did this for what she calls "self defense". I think it's a great analogy. I've tried to explain arbitrage to my friends and family and most of them have absolutely no idea what I'm talking about. It can be tiring to try to explain this business model over and over again, so now, in self defense, she can hand them a book that explains all of the details of FBA. Then, if they still have questions, she'll be happy to explain further.

Her website and book can be found here:

FBAStepByStep.com

Website, blog, and one-on-one mentoring service from Cynthia Stine.

Cynthia's book titled *Make Thousands on Amazon in 10 Hours a Week!* Available from Amazon: http://www.amazon.com/dp/061557548X/

Do you have a great idea for a website? Do you think you could write a book? **I say GO FOR IT!** Both Phyllis and Cynthia made their websites on their own and wrote their own books. A few short years ago they had no idea what FBA was, and now they have their own FBA websites and are both published authors!

All it takes is some **passion** and some **hustle**.

Chapter 12 – The Rules of the Amazon Marketplace

This is a short chapter but if you don't read this one, your tenure as an Amazon.com seller may be even shorter.

Whenever you wonder why Amazon does something, ask yourself this question: **does it provide a great experience for the Amazon buyer?** This is the key behind all Amazon programs and policies. Want proof? Amazon puts NEGATIVE product reviews on their site. Why? So that the buyer can make an informed decision and have a great buying experience on Amazon. Sure, Amazon could put all positive reviews on everything and see a short-term boost in sales, but it would affect their long-term goals of providing a great experience to the buyer. If a product fails for 90% of the buyers after two months of use but Amazon only showed the positive reviews from the 10% of the satisfied customers, then 9 out of 10 customers are going to have a poor buying experience and may not choose Amazon as their online retailer of choice for their next purchase.

If you are curious as to how this has worked out for Amazon, just take a look at their success and growth!

This policy should be seen as optimal for not just Amazon and the Amazon buyer, but also for anyone selling on Amazon! When you have a marketplace that has the best, most loyal customers who choose the Amazon marketplace FIRST and REPEATEDLY for their online purchases, you have a great place to sell your products! This environment is conducive to sellers who provide the best experience to the buyer. Good sellers, good buyers, good relationships, good business.

Amazon has spent many years and many dollars building this culture of trust and loyalty and they will protect it. There are policies in place to weed out sellers who do not meet the high standards that Amazon expects out of all of their sellers.

THIS IS VERY IMPORTANT SO I AM TYPING IN ALL CAPITAL LETTERS

You have to know and understand the rules of selling on Amazon, and especially FBA. Amazon is much different from eBay where you can mess up and eBay pretty much isn't going to do anything about it. Amazon is extremely customer focused and they have many rules in place that ensure that third party sellers provide Amazon customers with a high level of service. If these rules are not followed, then the customer may have a poor buying experience and that is the last thing that Amazon wants. If you're caught breaking Amazon's rules or provide a poor customer experience, Amazon will ban your account. I'm not talking about ban as in 'just go open another account with a different email address and they'll never know', I'm talking block all new accounts from your IP address, and anything tied to your credit cards or bank accounts. Ignorance of the rules is not an excuse with Amazon. The rules are there for you to read and when you create a seller account on Amazon, you are agreeing to follow those rules.

Compare this policy to eBay where providing a poor buying experience to the buyer simply means that you will likely get lower sales prices or fewer sales. If you want to take bad pictures, include a poor description, and offer restricting return policies, then you can. EBay will let you do this without penalty. They will recommend that you take good pictures, include detailed and accurate descriptions, and offer favorable return policies, in order to get more sales and at higher prices, but they don't make you do this. It's up to the seller to choose how professionally that they want to run their eBay business.

This difference in the buying experience has brought a lot of buyers, and subsequently sellers, over to the Amazon marketplace.

This is not meant to scare you. It is meant to make sure that you take selling on Amazon seriously. Before you jump in with both feet, read the Amazon rules for sellers. If you are unclear on something, ask questions online or contact Amazon. They have email and phone support. They want you to succeed, but if you are going to play in Amazon's sandbox, you will follow the Amazon rules.

Amazon is so passionate about customer service that they will even block new sellers in the Toys & Games category going into the fourth quarter (Christmas selling season). Don't worry, new sellers who use FBA are excluded; another perk of FBA! Wouldn't blocking new sellers reduce their profits and their bottom line? Possibly, but Amazon is not going to let some new seller start listing on Amazon in a category that sees a huge spike in sales and take a chance on that seller not delivering the promised goods to the customer. A new seller may get overwhelmed with the process and ship orders late, or offer items that they later find out that they can't fulfill and be forced to cancel orders. It's also possible that a new seller is someone who is trying to take advantage of the huge surge in fourth quarter sales to try to get away with fraudulent activity. Whatever the case, it poses a risk of a poor customer experience. Amazon is not going to take this risk as they would rather ensure the integrity of the Amazon marketplace than try to bump their bottom line every chance that they can. I applaud them for this as it builds a stronger customer base that has confidence to continue to buy from Amazon time and time again. It also keeps sellers out who are not able to perform at the high standards that Amazon requires. This is a good thing for existing sellers as well as keeping Amazon's business growing, which, in return, benefits third party sellers.

If you are selling using FBA, you have less to worry about compared to merchant fulfilled sellers. If you are 100% FBA, then you can't really ship something late because Amazon is doing the shipping. You can't be penalized for canceling orders because Amazon is managing your inventory levels. Just label your inventory properly, price your items competitively, and describe your items accurately and you're pretty much in the clear (still, read the rules!).

Even if something does get messed up like the seller gets the wrong item or the shipment arrived later than the expected delivery date, if it is an

Amazon order, Amazon will take responsibility. This includes removing any negative feedback that is related to the fulfillment experience (imagine eBay doing that!).

Here are the reasons that Amazon will remove negative feedback:

The feedback includes obscene language.

The feedback includes personally identifiable information.

The entire feedback comment is a product review.

The entire feedback comment is regarding fulfillment or customer service for an order fulfilled by Amazon. (Feedback which qualifies for removal under this rule will not be removed, but a line will appear through the rating and the statement, "This item was fulfilled by Amazon, and we take responsibility for this fulfillment experience" will be added.)

If you sell used books and media items where you have to select a condition other than 'New', then you have the possibility of receiving negative feedback if the buyer disagrees with your grading of the item. For this reason, I've always recommended grading very conservatively in order to give your buyer something that exceeds their expectations.

If you are 100% FBA and only sell items in 'New' condition, then it is actually pretty hard to get negative feedback. Still, it will happen. When it does, do what you can to keep the customer happy. You can contact them through the Amazon website and if you are able to rectify the situation you can ask them to consider removing their negative feedback. Good customer service will pay off (just look what it's done for Amazon!) and maintaining a high feedback rating will inspire greater buyer confidence and attract more buyers.

Under no circumstances should you only offer customer service or offer to return an item in exchange for removing negative feedback. Run your business as a professional and take your customer service seriously. Take care of any issues and only after the customer is satisfied should you ask them to consider removing negative feedback.

The Amazon A-to-Z Guarantee

http://www.amazon.com/gp/help/customer/display.html?ie=UTF8&nodeId=537868

From Amazon:

> What is the Amazon.com A-to-Z Guarantee?
>
> We want you to buy with confidence anytime you purchase products on the Amazon.com website or use Amazon Payments. That is why we guarantee purchases from Amazon Marketplace and Merchant sellers when payment is made via the Amazon.com website or when you use Amazon Payments for qualified purchases on third-party websites. The condition of the item you buy and its timely delivery are guaranteed under the Amazon A-to-Z Guarantee.

The Amazon A-to-Z Guarantee is the buyer's ultimate protection against a seller who may not be following the Amazon rules. You do not want to have A-to-Z Guarantee claims opened against you. This should be used as a buyer's last resort so a seller should have had ample time to correct any customer service issues with the buyer prior to the claim being opened. There are many types of A-to-Z Guarantee claims, but here is an example to show you that Amazon means business:

If you list a toy like a Star Wars Lego set on Amazon, you can't put in your description notes something like, "most of the pieces are there, and Darth Vader is missing. AS IS." This is not eBay where the listing for the item is what it is. On Amazon, you are listing on a specific product page and your item better match that description 100%. If a buyer received this partial Lego set and opened an A-to-Z Guarantee claim against you as a seller, you would not only lose and be forced to issue the buyer a full refund, but the buyer would not have to return the Lego set to you. Ouch.

How do you avoid A-to-Z Guarantee claims? Simple; follow the rules! Read them and follow them. I have never had an A-to-Z Guarantee claim opened against me and I don't plan to ever let that happen. I'm sure Amazon also keeps track of A-to-Z Guarantee claims against sellers and could ban a seller if they receive too many.

There are lots of rules and there is not enough space to list and discuss them all in here. The current Selling on Amazon rules can be found here:

http://www.amazon.com/gp/help/customer/display.html/ref=hp_sn_sell ?nodeId=1161232

Here is a link to the FBA homepage:

http://www.amazonservices.com/content/fulfillment-by-amazon.htm

Chapter 13 - Sales Rank Explained – What It Is, What It Is Not

Products listed for sale on Amazon have what is called a Sales Rank, or more recently, a Bestsellers Rank. One thing to always remember is that Amazon does not have to provide this information. Currently they do provide it and it is a piece of data that sellers can use to decide the products they want to stock and sell on Amazon, either through FBA, or by shipping their orders themselves.

There is a lot of bogus information out there about what Sales Rank means. Many sites will tell you that Sales Rank will tell you how fast an item will sell. This is not true at all. They will say that an item with a lower Sales Rank (lower being better as in the #1 seller is better than the #100 seller) will sell faster or is a 'better seller' than the other. Again, simply not true.

Sales Rank is actually very simple. It is an indication of recent sales. Nothing more.

Now that you know what Sales Rank is, how do you use this piece of information? How can you decipher the data at your disposal to make the best buying decision? This is what I want to teach you.

Sales Rank Means Different Things in Different Categories.

There are a lot more books listed for sale on Amazon than there are toys. At the time of writing this book, there are 39,397,115 book listings and only 2,578,142 toy listings. So a book with a 100K Sales Rank is in the top 0.25% of all book listings. A toy with a Sales Rank of 100K is in the top 3.9%. Huge difference (15X+) as you can see. You have to read Sales Rank differently in different categories.

When Items Don't Sell, Sales Rank Gets Higher and Higher and Higher...

If an item has not sold in a long time, then the Sales Rank will gradually get higher and higher until the item sells again. Try to think of Sales Rank this way; when an item sells on Amazon, the Sales Rank will 'spike'. If you were charting Sales Rank over time on a graph, you would see a literal spike in the graph.

Here's a simple and inexpensive experiment that you can run to test this and see for yourself. Find a high ranking item sold through FBA. Make a note of the Sales Rank at the time that you purchase it. Then watch the Sales Rank jump (Amazon updates Sales Rank every hour). You'll see that high-ranking item all of a sudden has a good Sales Rank!

A book that hasn't sold a single copy in two years may have a Sales Rank of over 2 million. Buy it once and it spikes to 80K, for ONE SALE. One sale in TWO YEARS. Now compare that to the book that has sold one copy every month for the past two years. It may have a Sales Rank of 80K and it has sold one copy a month, every month, for two years. So twenty-four copies compared to one copy. SAME SALES RANK. Is it starting to make sense now? Sales Rank is just a snapshot in time.

Real World Examples

Here is a graph of Sales Rank tracked over a period of one week. You can see how it climbs slowly and then drops dramatically. This happens when the item SELLS. I also refer to this as a spike in Sales Rank.

Sales Rank Graph for this Period:

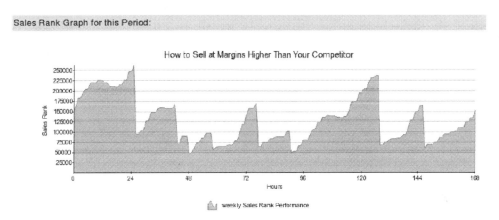

Here is the same graph, but I have enhanced the changes in Sales Rank to line up with the item's sales. This book sold eight copies this week.

Sales Rank Graph for this Period:

Here is another interesting graph of my first book. This graph is over the period of one week when I dropped the Amazon price from $25 to $9.95. You can see exactly how the Sales Rank changes due the increased sales volume.

Here is the same data over the entire month.

How To Use Sales Rank

When you decide what items to buy to sell on Amazon, you should use Sales Rank as one piece of information that you have at your disposal. You should also look at the item itself. If you scan a 1994 tax planner guide that comes back with a 'good Sales Rank' of 100K, should you buy it without thinking or should you stop and consider all of the dynamics at play. The book has a Sales Rank of 100K. This only means that it has sold one copy recently. Nothing more. Who bought it? Who knows? Several scenarios come to mind. Maybe it was purchased by mistake? Maybe a buyer has $31 in their Amazon shopping cart and needed a $4 FBA book to get to $35 for Free Super Saver Shipping? (This can be cheaper than paying shipping on a $31 order.) Who knows? Do you really think someone is going to buy it again? You should look at the market price vs. your cost to determine if the margin is high enough to warrant the risk of laying out inventory dollars for the item. This is where you can make the judgment call with your head that while it may have a recent sale, it will likely not sell again for a long time.

You may be asking, "Wouldn't items with lower Sales Ranks be better items to sell?" The answer is yes, but let me explain why the answer is yes. Items with a low Sales Rank mean that they have sold recently. The lower the rank, the more frequently they have sold recently. Think spike after spike after spike, each time getting a better and better Sales Rank. This is a good indication that the items will sell again. This is why lower Sales Rank items are generally considered 'better' to sell on Amazon.

Always remember that just because something has been selling well, doesn't mean it will always continue to sell well. Think about fads that come and go. They may be selling like crazy one month and dead in the water the next. Many items are also seasonal, meaning they sell well during some times of the calendar year, and perhaps not at all during other times. Think Christmas lights.

You can use all the data at your disposal, including Sales Rank, to evaluate items but it is ultimately up to you to learn how to read that data and how to use it to lower your risk and help you make the best buying decisions.

Real World Examples

I have an item on Amazon and I created the listing using a purchased UPC. I'm the only one who has ever sold this item. I get the emails when they ship out. We don't sell a ton, but I check Sales Rank every now and then. I've seen it as low as 4K and as high as 40K. So is it a 4K item? Or a 40K item? I sold fifty units in five months, so say ten a month or one every three days. Even with a steady sales rate OVER TIME, the Sales Rank fluctuates tremendously between sales. 4K Sales Rank would be after selling two in one day. 40K Sales Rank would be after not selling any for a week or more. This product is listed in the Office Products category on Amazon.

Another item I sell for which I created the product page took two months to get the first sale. I have been the only seller of this item (and still am). This item is in the Home Improvement category. It went from 0 Sales Rank to 14K Sales Rank. A week later it was at 70K Sales Rank. Two weeks later, 90K Sales Rank. It will sink lower until it sells again at which time it will spike to 10K-14K Sales Rank and then slowly drop again until the next sale.

It has sold one unit in the entire history of Amazon (although you could say in three months). Say you scanned this item and the margins were attractive. Was it a good item when the Sales Rank was at 14K? But not a week later when it's at 70K? Do you see why you cannot let Sales Rank dictate what you buy and don't buy? Will it ever sell again? Probably, but Sales Rank has nothing to do with it. Sales Rank will continue to climb (sink?) as other items sell and jump above its Sales Rank. When it sells again, it will jump up and then slide back down.

Here is another example from the Home Improvement category:

Sold item on 6/30/11, in the Home Improvement category. This was a merchant fulfilled item. I am the only seller and have been the only seller since I created the product page.

As soon as I got the email, I checked Sales Rank. It was 170,999. A little later, it was 9,183. Same item has a Sales Rank of 170K one hour and the next hour the Sales Rank is at 9K. This is a huge difference over just one sale.

If you base buying decisions only on Sales Rank, is this a bad item in the morning but a good item in the afternoon?

More Data to Consider

Last time I sold this item was 6/5/11. So it took 25 days of no sales to get to 170K. So for simplicity, say this item sells once a month, every month. An item with this sell through rate can have a Sales Rank as high as 170K and as low as 9K (and anywhere in between) depending upon when you look at the item.

The 10 Million Ranked Book

Bob Willey from the FBAForum Yahoo Group sold a book that he forgot that he had listed. It was listed as a merchant fulfilled book and he listed it almost three years prior to the sale. Once he received the email that it had sold, he checked the Sales Rank. It was 10,042,312! He emailed me after he received the order and I anxiously waited to see the new Sales Rank based on this single sale. It jumped to 94,060 after JUST ONE SALE.

Bob listed this book on 5/23/08 and it sold on 7/18/11 so it took over three years to sell. There is no telling how long it will take to sell again.

I hope this explanation and these examples help your business use Sales Rank appropriately to make the best buying decisions.

What About Items With No Sales Rank?

You'll eventually run across items with no Sales Rank and you'll wonder why. There are actually many reasons why an item will not have a Sales Rank.

It could be that the item has never sold in the history of Amazon.

It could be that Amazon has assigned the item a sub-category Sales Rank but not an overall Sales Rank.

It could be that the item is in a category that does show Sales Ranks.

It could be that the item is selling well, but Amazon, at their discretion, simply decides not to give the item a Sales Rank.

It could be that Amazon's computer systems are not displaying Sales Rank at the point in time that you are looking (and it will come back later).

When you have a true understanding of Sales Rank, you'll be able to identify these scenarios and still be able to make buying decisions.

Most Amazon sellers do not possess this level of knowledge about what Sales Rank truly means. By learning this information, you'll have and enjoy a competitive advantage over them.

The Top 5% of a Category

I've read about sellers calculating the Sales Rank cut off for items that are in the 'Top 5%' of each category. This sounds like a good idea to try to determine the most popular items in each category on Amazon. Personally, I discourage this practice because Sales Rank and the number of different listings in each category are simply not related.

I ran the numbers for the book and toy categories using real numbers from September 2011 to July 2012.

September 2011
Books: 32,000,410 listings
Toys: 963,514 listings
Top 5% of books: under 1.6 MILLION
Top 5% of toys: under 48,000

July 2012
Books: 39,397,115 listings
Toys: 2,578,142 listings
Top 5% of books: under 1.97 MILLION
Top 5% of toys: under 129,000

So because of the increased number of listings (not necessarily new items that are selling), the top 5% cutoff rises. It will continue to rise month after month and year after year.

Remember, these two pieces of information are not related. As more time goes by, there will be more and more listings in each Amazon category. This does not mean that sellers should be raising their Sales Rank cutoff guidelines. If there was 80 million book listings, would the new cutoff be items with a Sales Rank under 4 million? It doesn't make sense because the two pieces of information are not related. Sales Rank is merely an indicator of recent sales and is not related to how many items are listed in the specific Amazon category.

Here is some more information about the same product mentioned earlier in this chapter in the Office Products category. Since I've been the only seller of this item ever, I can track its history. I know for a fact that it has not sold in 14 months. At the time of this writing, it has a Sales Rank of 114,570. There are 2,256,468 items in the Office Products category meaning that this item is still in the top 5% of the category despite not selling on over a year. Do you really want to stick to the top 5% of a category if it means some items haven't sold a single unit in over a year? Long Tail items are one thing, but your money may be better invested in faster turning inventory.

Consider the book category. I've seen Sales Ranks in the 10 millions, but there are almost 40 million book listings. That means that ¾ of all book listings have no Sales Rank at all, likely because they have never sold in the history of Amazon.

Sales Rank can seem complex and with an improper understanding of what it actually means, a seller can easily misinterpret its meaning which can lead to poor buying decisions. Use Sales Rank wisely and as just one piece of the puzzle when evaluating items for resale. There are many factors to consider (other than Sales Rank) that can be much more important and relevant such as margin and competition.

Chapter 14 – The Amazon Buy Box

The Amazon Buy Box is a highly coveted place because the majority of Amazon sales go to sellers who have the Buy Box. It is the most visible placement on Amazon and this makes it the most likely that buyers will purchase the item from that particular sellers.

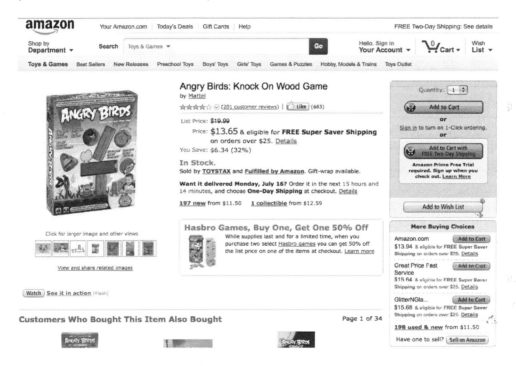

Exactly how to get the Buy Box is not fully known, but through experimentation it is generally agreed upon that Amazon sellers who are within less than 2% of the lowest price (price + shipping) and have Featured Merchant status are eligible for the Buy Box. These eligible sellers will rotate through the Buy Box at different times.

You're likely now wondering how to attain Featured Merchant status and just like the exact criteria for winning the Buy Box is not fully known, neither are the exact criteria for becoming a Featured Merchant.

Amazon has their Featured Merchant guidelines published here:

http://www.amazon.com/gp/help/customer/display.html?nodeId=200418180

Featured Merchants are Pro Merchant sellers who have met performance-based requirements. There is no additional fee for being a featured merchant, and sellers must maintain their performance levels in order to retain the status of Featured Merchant. Sellers with Featured Merchant status gain placement advantages for their listings on Amazon.com. Their listings are eligible to compete for the Buy Box and listings that do not win the Buy Box are eligible for placement in the More Buying Choices box.

Featured Merchant Qualifications

Sellers are evaluated based on factors that have been carefully chosen in an effort to give customers the best shopping experience. Featured Merchant status is evaluated based on the following criteria:

-ODR (Order Defect Rate)--ODR is based on customer feedback, A-to-z claims and chargebacks
-Other seller performance metrics
-Customer shopping experience offered on an item, such as speed of delivery, shipping options, price, and 24x7 customer service (including through the seller's participation in Fulfillment by Amazon)
-Time and experience on the Amazon selling platform
-Status as a Pro Merchant

Basically, if do everything that you should be doing such as describing your items accurately, shipping your orders on time, and answering your customer service emails in a timely fashion, you'll likely attain Featured Merchant status quite easily. It is even easier to attain if you use FBA because all of your orders are guaranteed to ship on time.

Here is a close-up view of an Amazon product page. Amazon buyers basically have three ways to purchase an item.

1. The Amazon Buy Box

In this example, the Amazon seller TOYSTAX has the Buy Box. Most Amazon buyers will buy from the seller who gets the Buy Box.

2. Under More Buy Choices, there can be up to three offers from Amazon sellers with Featured Merchant status.

In this example, Amazon is listed under More Buying Choices and not in the Buy Box.

3. New & Used Link

This is where all of the other marketplace offers will be listed.

You can see that it less likely that an Amazon buyer is going to click through to see the other offers, even of some of those offers are at a lower price than the seller who has the Buy Box.

It is for this reason that many Amazon sellers compete fiercely for the Buy Box. It can mean a huge surge in sales when you have the Buy Box on a popular item.

Learning a Lesson

A story was published online about an Amazon seller who was frustrated about their struggles competing with Amazon. They had been selling an item for $29.99 and they were selling about 100 per week. Then Amazon started to carry the product and their sales dropped to about 20 per week.

First, this number is interesting. The sales rate of this item likely did not change when Amazon started to sell it; it was likely still about 100 per week. Now that Amazon was a seller, it looks like the Amazon buyer prefers to buy from Amazon about 80% of the time when the price is the same from other marketplace sellers (this is a very unscientific assumption based on only one data point).

The story continued that the seller started to drop price in order to compete with Amazon. Amazon also dropped their price and they eventually got to a level where the seller was unable to compete and they stopped selling the item.

There are several lessons to be learned here.

First, be very careful when trying to compete against Amazon (there are strategies listed in the bonus chapter #1 at the end of this book).

Second, note that it was the seller who initiated the pricing war with Amazon. They should have been happy with their 20% of the total sales.

Third, the case can be made that all things being equal, including price, most of the time the Amazon buyer will buy from Amazon over a third party seller.

More Buy Box Information

Amazon has a lot of great information online on how the Buy Box works:

http://www.amazon.com/gp/help/customer/display.html?nodeId=20040 1830

I've pulled out the highlights to be aware of.

Sellers must qualify for Featured Merchant status in order to compete for Buy Box placement. Featured Merchant status is tied to specific seller performance criteria that determine the sellers who have consistently provided customers with a great buying experience on the Amazon.com site.

The Buy Box winner for a product is selected from the pool of eligible sellers offering that product based on, among other things, price and availability. Amazon will present the winning seller's "New" offering as the first choice for buyers using the "Add to Shopping Cart" box on product detail pages. For many sellers, this placement may lead to increased product sales.

Chapter 15 – Risk Management

Every item that you purchase for resale will represent some degree of risk. After all, there are no guarantees that any item will ever sell again. Even the number one selling book has the possibility of completely dropping off in sales.

The idea is to use as much information as possible that you have at your disposal to make the best buying decisions. The better your information, the better buying decisions that you'll make, and the lower your risk will be.

Because you don't know exactly what has sold before, you have to use the information that you do have access to in order to make good buying decisions. This data includes Sales Rank, competition, margin, and good old-fashioned intuition.

Sales Rank

In the previous chapter we talked about what Sales Rank is as well as what it isn't. When an item has a good Sales Rank, that means that it has had recent sales. Recent sales are a good indicator that the item will sell again (but are not a guarantee).

Amazon Sales Histories

Amazon does not provide any histories of their sales. This policy comes from their legal department so I would not hold out on seeing anything like this anytime soon.

Competition

You can also use your competition to gauge if an item should be sold online. If there are a lot of sellers, especially FBA sellers and the margin is good on the item, then it's more than likely a good item to sell online. Why? Well, you are using the fact that multiple other sellers also believe it to be a good product to sell online. You can piggyback on their knowledge, or at least use it to help you make your buying decision. Again, this is not a guarantee as there will be instances where multiple sellers are all selling a dud item.

Margin

Always consider margin when deciding what to buy. If the item has a large margin of profit, then you have more room to take risks. If the item has less margin, then you want to make sure that the item will sell quickly. The amount of margin in an item can dramatically alter your buying decisions. Remember, you're going to find items at steep discounts that will have high margin for you but that other sellers are selling with lower margin because their costs were higher. These are all things to consider when managing your risk when making buying decisions.

Risk vs. Reward

It all comes down to risk versus reward. If the reward is great, you should be willing to take higher risks. If the reward is smaller, you should take smaller risks.

No one is going to hit a home run every single time, so don't gauge the success of your business this way. Home runs are great, but singles, doubles and triples are also profitable. You'll even have some strikeouts products that you wish you'd never purchased in the first place. **Don't let the fear of possible buying a dud keep you from getting in this game!**

If your margins are high and your costs are low, it can be fun and financially rewarding to take some risks. If they sell, you get a nice profit, but if they don't you are not in a position to lose a lot of money. One great sale like this can pay for lots of additional "gambles".

On the other side of this, if the reward is small (lower margins), then the risk had better be small. If you are used to 100% margins but you find a high quantity of an item that has 50% margins, it may be an attractive deal to resell if the other factors indicate that the item will sell quickly. **If you can get in, get paid, and get out with low risk, then the lower margins can make sense.**

Just don't play mind games with yourself and think too hard about each and every deal. There are too many deals out there! If you don't have a good feeling about an item, put it back and move on. Don't tie up your inventory dollars in items that you do not have confidence in. Selling online is completely scalable meaning that you can start small and grow at your own pace.

You'll end up finding good deals and great deals. Unless you have unlimited funds with which to buy inventory, you should be spending your money on the great deals and be disciplined enough to leave the good deals behind.

Chapter 16 – It's a Margins Game

This book is listed in the Recommended reading section at the end of this book:

How to Sell at Margins Higher Than Your Competitors

By Lawrence L. Steinmetz & William T. Brooks

It will change the way that you see price, competition, and margin. When selling on Amazon as a reseller, you have to consider margin above all other factors. You've probably heard people say that 'they'll just make it up in volume.' This is a recipe for disaster when you stop, sit down, and run the numbers. Here is a simplified example that they use in this book:

Consider a business that makes a product on which they enjoy a 35% margin. It costs them $65 to produce and they sell it for $100. They do an even $1,000,000 in sales in order to break even. Their margin covers the entire business overhead including salaries.

These simplified numbers mean that they spend $650,000 on producing 10,000 units with a cost of $65 each. The margin of 35% or the profit of $35 on those 10,000 equates to $350,000 to cover overheads.

This is their break-even point. While they are not turning a profit, they are not losing money and providing employment to their workers.

If the CEO all of a sudden says that they want to lower price and cut margins and attempt to 'make it up in volume' with no other business plan for sustainable growth, here is what will happen. Everyone at the company will work twice as hard and make no additional profit.

The complete breakdown is explained in detail in the book but what you will find is that in this example with these numbers, by cutting their price by 10%, they will have to do double their work to make and sell twice as many units in order to make the same amount of money and break even.

Conversely, if they raised price by 10%, they could sell one-third less (lose one-third of their sales), do one-third less work, and make the same amount of money.

For some reason, many struggling retailers who, in a last ditch effort to get back on track, try to lower prices and make it up in volume. Does it ever work? Nope. All of those struggling retailers are now out of business.

It's Always About Margin

Understanding margin is easily the biggest thing that you need to learn in order to stay in business when selling online. If you fail to understand margin, you will end up working too hard for too little money and eventually go out of business. There's really no way around it.

From Wikipedia: http://en.wikipedia.org/wiki/Profit_margin

Profit margin, net margin, net profit margin or net profit ratio all refer to a measure of profitability. It is calculated by finding the net profit as a percentage of the revenue.

Net Profit Margin = (Net Income / Revenue) x 100

Where Net Income = Revenue - Cost

Profit margin is an indicator of a company's pricing strategies and how well it controls costs.

The terms Margin and Markup have technically different definitions, but both are used to indicate the profitability of an item in terms of a percentage.

http://en.wikipedia.org/wiki/Markup_%28business%29

Markup is the difference between the cost of a good or service and its selling price. A markup is added on to the total cost incurred by the producer of a good or service in order to create a profit. The total cost reflects the total amount of both fixed and variable expenses to produce and distribute a product. Markup can be expressed as a fixed amount or as a percentage of the total cost or selling price. Retail markup is commonly calculated as the difference between wholesale price and retail price, as a percentage of wholesale. Other methods are also used.

Assume the sale price is $100 and the cost is $25

Markup = ($100 - $25) / $25 = 300%

To convert from markup to profit margin:

Profit Margin = (Sale price - Cost) / Sale price

($100 - $25) / $100 = 75%

Keep your margins and your markups high! This is to protect yourself in the event of changing market conditions such as price drops due to increased competition or simply price erosion over time.

When you learn the vital importance of margin and price over volume, you'll learn to protect price and margin and work smart while your competition works hard.

An example that I like to use is when you hear people talk about how much money they make online. Someone may make the claim that they made $100,000 and how awesome they are and laugh at someone who only made $50,000. What they forget is that it is not the total profit that makes a business successful or not; it's the effort behind those profits. It's not a fair comparison when a seller who makes $100,000 profit on high volume, low margin items compares themselves to a seller who makes $50,000 with low volume, high margin items. When they claim that they are so much better because they made twice as much money, I would tell them that they should have made TEN TIMES as much money because they actually worked TEN TIMES harder!

I remember talking to a new seller who created a new product page on Amazon and had received her first few sales. She was making $10 profit on each one that sold. She was thrilled! She thought this was an easy $10. I asked her what her margins were and she admitted to having no idea. I asked her what her cost was on the item, and she was hesitant to say. She finally admitted that her cost was $100. $100 to make $10! Some sellers may be happy with this, but I would not be. I would rather have my $100 tied up in inventory that was giving me a much better return than $10.

Here are the numbers (simplified):

Assume the sale price is $110 and the cost is $100

Markup = ($110 - $100) / 100 = 10%

To convert from markup to profit margin:

Profit Margin = (Sale price - Cost) / Sale price

($110 - $100) / $110 = 9.1%

I asked her what she was planning to do if she had to take one return from an unsatisfied customer that could not be resold. I think she saw the light at this point; she'd have to sell ten more just to break even! $1100 in sales and $1000 out of pocket for inventory for zero dollars in profit? No thanks!

Do you need any more reasons to keep your margins high? How about accounting for returns? If you sell enough stuff online, you will get returns. If your margins on a product line are low, a few returns can wipe out your entire profit on the entire line of products!

A certain amount of returns should be accounted for in your margin calculations. In fact, all scenarios should be accounted for in your margin calculations! The big retailers do this, and so should you. Home Depot knows that a certain percentage of a product will be stolen from their stores, destroyed by forklifts, under-shipped by vendors, incorrectly received by the store, lost in the overhead, stolen by employees, used for in store projects, among other things.

Many of these scenarios are what's more commonly called 'shrink'. Retailers account for it so that there are no surprises. They KNOW these things will happen so they simply account for it financially.

This is why you keep your margins high. Do I really think that you need to factor in a half percentage to your margins in the event that a rogue UPS driver steals your inbound FBA shipments? No, not really, but when your margins are high and healthy, any surprises that come along will not throw your entire business model upside down.

Chapter 17 – The 'Race to the Bottom' & 'Chasing the Next Sale'

There are two common phrases that you may start hearing when you are selling products online. These are the 'Race to the Bottom' and 'Chasing the Next Sale'. These are both the result of sellers who too often don't understand the marketplace dynamics at play and the factors that go into each buyer's decision-making process. They are the result of sellers who think that they can only compete on price and that price is king. They believe that the seller with the lowest price, even if only by $0.01, will be the only seller to get sales on Amazon.com. If you've read this far in the book, I hope that you see how this is simply not true. Buyers do not buy based on price alone and how cutting price is not a sustainable long-term business strategy.

As mentioned in Chapter 6, price, supply, and demand are constantly changing. Each time you look at the Amazon marketplace, you are only looking at a snapshot in time. As time goes by, things will change. Sellers will sell out, demand will rise and fall, supply will come and go and all the while price will be affected. Sometimes prices will go up and sometimes prices will go down.

Racing to the Bottom and Chasing the Next Sale are NOT strategies that I recommend. I want you to understand what causes these things to happen so that you do not get caught up in a downward spiral that negatively affects your margins and profits.

The Race to the Bottom

The race to the bottom happens when sellers repeatedly undercut each other in an attempt to be the lowest price. It's a shame that this happens because so many buyers do not buy based on price alone, so sellers who repeatedly undercut only hurt their own businesses.

This can also happen when multiple sellers use automated repricing programs. The sellers may have poorly implemented pricing rules without safeguards to prevent lowering prices too much, or the repricing programs themselves are just poorly designed and written. These programs can go off in succession and result in a downward spiral of price, margins, and profits. A profitable item can be reduced to not profitable in a very short amount of time for no good reason other than aggressive sellers competing to see who can make the LEAST amount of money. This is not a strategy that I promote for obvious reasons.

I suppose this is good for the buyers of these products, but this is not an attractive set of circumstances for sellers.

Smart sellers need to learn to avoid the race to the bottom and also be able to identify it when it happens. Some sellers will even buy up their entire competitors inventory when this happens and items are listed for sale well below the equilibrium market price. See how supply, demand, and price just always seem to work things out in the free market? ☺

Chasing the Next Sale

Chasing the next sale happens when sellers don't stop to consider that items will sell throughout the year. It sounds very simple and logical that items will sell throughout the year and that a product is not just going to sell one more unit and then never sell again, doesn't it? You'd never know it the way that some sellers compete so aggressively on price. They are determined to be the absolute lowest price and 'chase' that next sale. They will lower their price (and reduce their margins) in order to undercut any and all competitors until the item sells.

I believe this to be a shortsighted strategy. It may be an item that sells 300 units every month on Amazon.com. Does it really matter if you are the first sale of the month or the last? What is the incredible motivation to be the 'next' sale? Personally, I prefer to sell at higher margins when I make the sale. When you stop and consider the number of units of each product that will sell on Amazon.com each month, being overly concerned with who is able to get the 'next sale' starts to sound pretty silly.

Some sellers will even lower their prices to levels where they are actually losing money on every sale just to be 'the next sale'. I'd rather not sell at all than sell items like this. $0 profit is $0 profit, but it is more profit than taking a loss on an item. If you see other sellers doing this, just leave them alone. Let them sell out at their low prices. Time will tell which sellers will remain in business.

Real World Pricing Example

I was working with an ScanPower user over the phone and we were also using remote screen sharing software so I could watch what she was doing. She was getting used to the ScanPower workflow as I walked her through it. Here's what happened next:

She entered a book and it showed that it had a Sales Rank of under 12,000 (this is a very good Sales Rank). She graded it VeryGood, and then came to the ScanPower pricing popup screen. The lowest merchant fulfilled net price was $9.95 in Acceptable condition. Amazon was selling it for $19.95. There was one other FBA seller in Good condition priced at $14.95. I thought for sure that she would click on the $14.95 FBA price but instead she clicked the $9.95 price. She wanted to match her FBA listing in VeryGood condition against a merchant fulfilled Acceptable condition offer.

I know, you're probably wondering what was she thinking. Don't worry; we were on the phone so I offered her some advice on pricing FBA items. I suggested that she match the $14.95 price and that it was pretty much a guaranteed sale at that price due to the popularity of the item and her specific condition compared to her competitors. This was a price 50% higher than the lowest price. I was surprised when she did not like my advice, after all, my advice was intended to help her make more margin and more profits on her inventory.

She started to tell me how I didn't know what I was talking about and how important it is to simply get the books listed and sold and how speed was everything and how she had no time to stop and look at prices and how she always just matches to total lowest price regardless of condition. Yikes! She was chasing the next sale on a 12,000-ranked book, and as an FBA seller no less! It seemed like I was in for some trouble, but I really wanted to help her learn to price her items well. I tried some simple explanations about understanding the Amazon buyer and the advantages that FBA sellers enjoy over their merchant fulfilling competitors. She did not want to hear it. She proceeded to tell me how she has been selling books online for three years and she knew what she was doing and the three seconds that I recommended she take to stop and look at the competitive pricing information was just too long and it would slow her down too much. I tried again with some helpful information about how it may only be a few dollars, but how it can really add up over time. She came back at me again telling me how she does $350,000 in sales every year and that she knows what she is doing and has no interest in any other pricing strategies.

I'll admit that my frustration level was rising a bit at this point although her bottom line didn't really affect me personally. In a pretty stern voice I told her that my advice would increase her prices, margins, and profits by an estimated 50% meaning an additional $175,000 on her $350,000 business. The phone was silent for a few seconds. I had finally gotten my point across. We finished our discussion on how to price FBA items and I'm happy to say that she is still a customer of ours and she is enjoying higher margins.

Chapter 18 – What Makes a Product Good for Resale

I'd rather teach you to fish than just give you a fish so in this chapter we're going to talk about why there are no lists of good products to sell online. **A product is not good for resale because it is on a list; it is good for resale because of all the factors surrounding that product.** If I had a list of products that were good for resale, it would benefit you more to learn WHY those products are on that list.

You have to learn this business and not just blindly follow every expert out there. This includes me as well! I want to teach you this business and how to use the required tools to become successful. It won't do either of us any good if I just tell you what to do and then you go do it without ever learning WHY this all works the way that it does. As soon as I stopped telling you what to do, your business would fail. This is not the position that I want to be in and it should not be a position that you want to find yourself in, either.

When you make buying decisions, you need to make them with confidence. You know the risks involved and the rewards that match those risks. Things to consider:

Margin

Personally, the number one thing that I consider is margin. Review Chapter 16 to be sure that you have the proper view of margin and volume. When margins are high, you can take more risks.

Competition (or lack thereof)

I always want to see the competition on an item. I want to know if there are other FBA sellers or if Amazon is selling the product. I want to look at the complete pricing picture so that I can make an educated guess at what the expected sales price or market price will be. Remember, it's not always about what the item is listed for, you need to have confidence in what it will actually sell for. You will find items where all of the sellers have priced an item non-competitively high and will never sell. I also want to see if there is no competition or even just no FBA competition. Being the only FBA seller is a powerful position to be in, especially if Amazon is also not selling the item. Remember the FBA Land Grab from Chapter 4?

Brand

Good, popular brands will have a better chance of having strong demand as well as lasting demand over time as people trust and prefer brands with good reputations.

Category/Type of Item

Some categories will be better to sell in than others. Consider the Toy category that was discussed in Chapter 9. Categories that have the same characteristics as the Toy category will respond in a similar way to the market forces of supply and demand.

Homeruns Or Singles?

A lot of sellers hear all of the homerun stories about buying 200 items for $5 each that are selling for over $100 on Amazon and while homeruns like that do happen if you are out in the stores and doing this business, they are rare. Don't think about only trying to hit homeruns. Just like in baseball, you'll score a lot more runs if you hit a lot of singles than if you only try to hit homeruns. The best part about this is that singles are easy and don't slow you down in your search for homeruns.

A deal isn't a deal just because someone says that it is a deal. There are so many things that can differ between two resellers looking at identical items. If the item sells online for $70 and one reseller finds it for $50, it's not a deal. But if another reseller finds it for $20, then it is a deal. So you can't just put items on a list, because you need to have a price point at which the product becomes a deal. Since every product can become a deal at a certain price point, the 'deal list' would be a list of every product ever! A list like this is not useful which is why you need to carry FBAScout for accurate data, learn this business, decide how you want to run your business and take action.

It's also a good idea to remember that some deals that you like will not be attractive to other sellers and that some sellers will buy things to resell that you would never consider selling. **That's OK!**

Different sellers have different business models, different risk tolerance levels, and different levels of funds to buy inventory. You should be able to scan items next to someone else, put different products in your carts, and then go have lunch together and stay friends.

Chapter 19 – Sourcing Products – Retail vs. Online

The subjects of sourcing products at retail and online are way too long to be included in this book, and not every online seller will be sourcing products at retail or online. I've written two other books that deal with in-depth strategies for retail and online sourcing called:

Retail Arbitrage: The BLUEPRINT for Buying Retail Products to Resell for BIG PROFITS

and:

Online Arbitrage: The BLUEPRINT for Buying Products Online to Resell for BIG PROFITS

Sourcing products is probably the number one topic that people want to talk about and it is obviously very important. There are many places to source inventory. In the previous chapter, we talked about what makes a product a good deal to sell online and how there is not just a list of products that are good to sell online. We'll take that a step further and discuss different sources of products and the advantages and disadvantages of both.

First thing that I want to mention is that there are big differences between retail stores and their online counterparts. Knowing these differences will allow you to properly evaluate the market dynamics at play. Knowledge is power and knowing the differences here can give you the information to find deals that your competition overlooks.

Home Depot vs. HomeDepot.com

I am very familiar with this relationship for reasons that you can probably guess from reading the beginning of this book. It may surprise you to know that Home Depot and HomeDepot.com are run completely separately. You cannot buy from HomeDepot.com and then return the product to your local Home Depot (at least not at the time of this writing). Products available at your local Home Depot may or may not be available on HomeDepot.com. Same thing for HomeDepot.com; they will carry products that are not available at your local Home Depot store.

How does knowing the differences help you as a reseller? Let me explain.

First, let's consider demand for certain products. You will undoubtedly see large-scale advertising campaigns on TV, on the radio and in print. These advertisements create demand for those products. Those products are only available in a limited supply for limited sales channels, namely Home Depot Stores or HomeDepot.com. Now add to this situation the dynamic that the product is also a house brand (discussed later in this chapter).

You now have demand for a product with limited distribution channels. Sure, HomeDepot.com can ship anywhere in the country and most of the population lives in close proximity to a Home Depot store, but consider these possibilities:

Customers who have never ordered a product online (and don't plan to start).

Customers who do not live near a Home Depot store.

Customers who are unaware of the house brand relationship so they look elsewhere for the product.

Neither HomeDepot.com nor Home Depot stores have unlimited supply of the product so when they sell out, supply is gone but demand remains. If you have some of that supply, you can now meet that demand and you are not bound by any pricing agreements. Your price is set by the simple market forces of supply and demand. Thanks to the Internet, you can offer your supply on several sites such as Amazon or eBay (shipping eBay orders through FBA is covered in Chapter 21).

Here's an example that surely plays out somewhere in the country:

A husband and wife are watching TV. The husband sees the Home Depot commercial and says to his wife that he would like that product for a Christmas gift. She makes a mental note and the next day goes on Amazon.com and purchases the product from an FBA seller. Done.

Why not go to Home Depot? Maybe she doesn't live near one. Maybe she didn't even realize it was a Home Depot commercial and she just remembered the product. Maybe Amazon is the first place that she considers for purchases. When she finds it on Amazon, she buys it and her shopping is done. Maybe going out shopping is the last thing that she wants to do.

Maybe she did note that it was from Home Depot but when she went to the store, she found out that they were sold out. Maybe she doesn't realize that HomeDepot.com even exists. Even if she did, HomeDepot.com may be sold out, or they may not even offer the product (some products are only sold in retail stores).

Once she finds it on Amazon for a price at which she values the item, she makes the purchase and the transaction takes place. She got what she wanted and the seller got what they wanted.

She may be paying more than retail in order to get her hands on a popular product that is not in stock at the regular MSRP. If she wants the item at this point in time, she has to pay the premium price on the secondary market. She may be paying this premium price knowingly or unknowingly. The facts of the matter are that price is set by supply and demand and a transaction only takes place when the buyer values the item more than the price and the seller values the price more than the item.

House Brands

House brands are brands that have partnerships in place with retailers. Some brands are even owned by the retailer. One of the most famous house brands is Craftsman tools. They are sold exclusively at Sears. I'm sure you are familiar with many brands that are called house brands, but you just didn't know that they were house brands. Ryobi tools at Home Depot is another house brand.

What happens is that these retailers like Sears and Home Depot put on their national advertising campaigns and create nationwide demand for their products. The supply is limited to certain channels such as the local stores and the company's website. There will be many reasons why the demand will not be able to reach the supply. Not everyone lives near a Sears and Sears.com may be sold out or not even carrying the product at all.

This goes for all kinds of products, not just power tools. It even works on grocery items. Have you heard of Trader Joe's? I use this example because it is easier to understand. If you haven't heard of Trader Joe's, I'll tell you this: People are crazy for Trader Joe's! It has very loyal shoppers who prefer their Trader Joe's branded products like salsa or olive oil. It is not unreasonable to assume that there are people out there who have a special preference for certain Trader Joe's products. Some of those people who at one time lived within shopping distance of a Trader Joe's have since relocated to another part of the country where there are no Trader Joe's. Now when they cook dinner, the only thing that they can think about is how they wish they had their special Trader Joe's olive oil. This is the DEMAND. They decide to go online and see if it's available from Amazon.com. THERE IT IS! You understood that this demand existed and you met that demand with your supply (if you live near a Trader Joe's) and you sent some supply to FBA. They are happy and purchase the olive oil, and you are happy and put the profit in your pocket.

This example doesn't work because it's Trader Joe's olive oil, it works because of the brand association, the dynamics of personal preference, and real world factors such as moving across the country. If you find other items that have these same characteristics, then you'll find more items that are good for arbitrage.

This strategy works for all kinds of products including Canadian exclusives. There are the same types of products available in Canada that Canadian buyers prefer. There are many Canadian ex-patriots living in the USA who shop on Amazon and prefer FBA sellers. If the products were made available on Amazon.com, they would purchase them. This is the DEMAND. You can meet this demand if you have access to the supply (either by importing in bulk or by living in Canada and using some creative FBA strategies discussed in the next chapter).

Examples of this type of supply and demand abound. Here is another one with a double twist; consider 'snowbirds' who live in the northern states during the summer and then travel to the southern states during the cold, harsh winters. They surely have favorite items that are only local to them during certain parts of the year. If you can provide the supply of those 'southern' items that they cannot get while they are up north or the 'northern' items that they cannot get while they are down south, then you are able to match up supply and demand with a profitable transaction. Supply and demand do not have to be very big when you have the power of the Internet bringing them together.

Retail Exclusives

There will be some products that are not sold online and are only sold as retail exclusives. There will be buyers (demand) who want these products (supply) who do not live near a store that sells them. These buyers may be more than happy to buy online if there was a seller selling the items. Out of all of the potential buyers who make up the total demand, some of them will value the item at a higher level than the others. Don't think that you have to sell to all of them; you just have to sell to the buyers who value the item the highest as long as this price that they are willing to pay is high enough to hit your target margins.

Retail deals are my favorite deals because you can find deals with sky-high margins and you are truly able to capitalize on knowledge being power. YOU know about the deal because YOU went out and found it.

You'll have less competition on deals like this, at least until someone else finds the same deal.

Online deals can be more risky because they are public and anyone can get in on them while the website still has supply to sell. This can lead to increased supply on the secondary market, which of course will drive prices down (at least temporarily).

Retail Advantages

Deals are only accessible to those who make the trip to the store.

Not everyone will be aware of the deals.

Low lead times; you can buy and list as merchant fulfilled the same day as well as buy and send to FBA in the same day.

Items can easily be returned if warranted.

Retail Disadvantages

Quantities can be limited.

Requires time and effort.

Online Advantage

Quantities can be higher than at retail (purchase 200 units instead of just 20 units).

You can purchase items and have them delivered to your door.

Online Disadvantages

Increased lead times (shipping time in transit) can lead to changed market dynamics by the time your products are available for sale.

Deals are 'public' meaning that anyone can find the deals and get in on them. This can increase the secondary market supply and drive down price.

The online returns process can be more difficult and cost money (return shipping).

For much more information about sourcing products for resale from retail stores as well as online, be sure to check out the books:

Retail Arbitrage: The BLUEPRINT for Buying Retail Products to Resell for BIG PROFITS

and:

Online Arbitrage: The BLUEPRINT for Buying Products Online to Resell for BIG PROFITS

All of my books can be found here: scanpower.com/books

Chapter 20 – International FBA & Advanced FBA Techniques

FBA is not just for US-based Amazon.com sellers. At the time of this writing, FBA is available in the USA, Japan, Germany, France, and the UK. You can bet Amazon has plans to roll out FBA in more countries soon.

FBA in Canada

Here is how you can sell on Amazon.com using FBA even if you are located in Canada. First, you need an Amazon.com seller account, a US bank account, a US credit card, and a US address (get a P.O. Box). All of these things can be done online. The easiest way is to get the credit card from the same bank where you open your US bank account. Once you have all of these pieces, you can open your US Amazon.com account just as if you were physically located in the US.

So even though you are in Canada, you can log into your Amazon.com account and prepare FBA shipments as though you were located in the US. You can even print UPS labels. But what address should you use for your 'Ship From' address? How will UPS charges be calculated?

Here's how to do it. Sellers have figured out that it is more cost-effective to print US postage from the US Post Office website at USPS.com and then physically take their shipments across the border. There are companies that have sprung up to help Canadian sellers get their online orders to their US customers. One of these companies that services the Toronto area is http://chitchatsexpress.com. For a fee, they will take bulk loads of shipments across the border for their customers. You can use services like this to get your US bound FBA shipments delivered through UPS as well.

Preparing FBA shipments that will be delivered to the US FBA warehouses will be prepared just like any other FBA shipments. You will need a US address for Amazon as a 'Ship From' address; Amazon will use this address to assign the fulfillment center and for UPS to calculate accurate inbound shipping charges. If you are using a border courier service, ask them what they recommend. They may be dropping off their shipments at a UPS store right over the border and you can use that store's address. If taking them over the border yourself, use the address of wherever you drop them off such as a UPS store or UPS drop off location.

This strategy works well for Canadian sellers who live near the border, but any seller can choose their own shipping service and send products to US FBA warehouses to be sold on Amazon.com. This also applies to any country where you can use FBA. US FBA sellers can send products to Japanese FBA warehouses and German FBA sellers can ship to UK FBA warehouses. The same account requirements exist for each country-specific Amazon seller account. Amazon even promotes this practice and will help you set up your international accounts. Use the Contact Amazon pages on each country-specific Amazon site if you need help getting your accounts set up.

You may have additional inbound shipping charges if you are getting your products to a US FBA warehouse from Canada or any other country. Take these additional costs into account when deciding what products to send to FBA.

The European Fulfilment Network (EFN)
(yes, they spell fulfillment differently over there)

This is starting to get pretty crazy.

An Amazon seller in the USA can prepare their inventory to be shipped to an Amazon warehouse in the UK where their items will then be made available to most European buyers. Amazon still stores, picks, packs, and ships the orders in Europe while the USA-based seller goes about their business.

This is a big step for many sellers so be sure that you've exhausted your domestic opportunities before taking the leap into using the EFN.

Due to the complexities with export, duties, taxes, etc., I recommend contacting Amazon when you're ready to make this step.

http://services.amazon.co.uk/landing-pages/amazon-europe-marketplaces-account/

Amazon Services Europe also did a webinar for US sellers who want to learn more about leveraging FBA and the EFN:

https://www1.gotomeeting.com/register/552193065

Direct to FBA

There is no reason why you have to be the one to send your products to your Amazon FBA account. Anyone can send products to your FBA account as long as they are prepared correctly and labeled properly. As your FBA business grows, you may find yourself working with suppliers who are willing to label your products for you and send them to your FBA account directly. They may have an integrated solution, or you may have to train them from scratch. FBA labels, packing slips, and UPS labels can all be saved as HTML files or PDFs and emailed to your supplier. You can even print them out yourself and send them to your supplier by UPS or USPS.

Risks

Finding companies that will send directly to your FBA account can be awesome because it eliminates duplicated shipping charges, reduces inbound shipping lead-time, and allows you to not have to be tied down to receive and process FBA inventory shipments. While there are rewards, there are also risks involved in a relationship like this.

These risks include:

Teaching your supplier how to use FBA and potentially inviting a new competitor

Losing a source of product if they decide to sell directly themselves

Trusting someone else to properly prepare your FBA inventory

In my experience, if you work with reputable companies, this type of relationship can be a real win-win. The risk that a company may decide to get into selling directly to consumers is real, but I think that you'll find that most companies do not want to add direct consumer sales to their businesses. There is a reason that so many companies do not sell directly to consumers and instead rely on distributors, wholesalers, and retailers to get their products to the end users. This is just not what they want to do; they are focused on other parts of their businesses.

If a company starts to sell directly, they stand to upset their other channels of distribution. Their wholesale channel and other distributors of their product may stop (or threaten to stop) selling their products in this case. Amazon is nice, but it is likely not their biggest sales channel so it would not be a smart move to risk everything just to sell on Amazon themselves.

FBA Global Export

Through this feature, you can export qualifying items in your FBA inventory including Books, Music, Videos, and DVDs (BMVD) and eligible non-media products using Priority (2-4 days), Expedited (5-8 days), and Standard (15-32 days, Media products only) shipping options from the U.S. to other countries.

Only Standard-Size Units are eligible for FBA Export. Oversize Units cannot be exported.

You can even use Multi-Channel Fulfillment (covered in more detail in the next chapter) for international orders! At the time of this writing, only BMVD inventory qualifies for International Multi-Channel Fulfillment.

Is it complicated to do all of this? Nope; it's as easy as enrolling in the FBA Global Export Program and uploading our signature and letting Amazon take care of the rest (packaging, shipping customs, etc.)

What will Amazon do next?

How will sellers being using FBA in the years to come? Only time will tell but I am optimistic and confident that Amazon will continue to be the place of amazing opportunities for those sellers who stay up to date on the latest changes and offerings. Most of the time it is the sellers who are first to act, first to move, or first to the market who will end up making the most money.

My Prediction

When it's all said and done, I believe that Amazon wants to have every product ever made available to anyone on the planet, anywhere on the planet, in two days or less.

Can Amazon do it? Time will tell.

Chapter 21 – Multi-Channel Fulfillment – List on eBay, Ship From FBA

Multi-Channel Fulfillment is an amazing tool that is often overlooked. Your FBA inventory is not locked to Amazon as a sales channel. You can still list on other sites and fulfill those orders with your FBA inventory. It is a common misconception that FBA is for Amazon only, and while Amazon and FBA certainly go hand-in-hand, a seller's items are not tied to the Amazon sales channel once they are stored in an FBA fulfillment center.

This chapter has two "Aha!" moments. The first is that you can ship your FBA inventory to fulfill orders that you receive from any channel such as eBay or your own website at very competitive rates (likely less than what it costs you to do it yourself). Using Multi-Channel Fulfillment allows you to sell on any sales channel and still fulfill your orders needing only access to a computer. You don't need to store your own inventory, multiple sizes of boxes, print labels, or go to the Post Office every day. You get the orders, and Amazon ships them out. This goes on whether you are at home or on vacation. Once you get your inventory to an FBA fulfillment center, you can manage it from anywhere on the planet! "Aha!"

The second is the big one; how to LEVERAGE this new information into increased margins and a more efficient business model. Using Multi-Channel Fulfillment properly can truly revolutionize your business. You can lower your overhead in shipping costs, labor costs, and warehouse costs, while at the same time increasing your margins on every item that you sell. This is because of the extremely competitive costs associated with Multi-Channel Fulfillment. I'll explain how to do this after the fee breakdown.

This is truly a win-win-win situation that most sellers would not believe is true:

Win #1: Increase margins and profits (higher payouts per item)

Win #2: Reduce work (outsource storage, picking, packing, and shipping)

Win #3: Improve customer satisfaction (shipments arrive faster)

This would seem like a magic potion from business fairly-land, but it's not; it's simply learning how to use the available tools optimally. Run the numbers (shown below) and take the steps to streamline your business.

Fees Involved

Yes, there are fees involved but these fees are fixed and known upfront for Multi-Channel Fulfillment orders. Since they are your orders and not orders on the Amazon website, there is no Amazon commission.

Multi-Channel Fulfillment Fees

The Multi-Channel Fulfillment fees consist of a per-order 'Order Handling' fee, a per-unit 'Pick & Pack' fee, and a per-pound 'Weight Handling' fee. These fees can be seen here:

Fees for Multi-Channel Fulfillment orders

Orders placed through other sales channels.

Shipping Method		Standard	Expedited (Two-Day)	Priority (Next-Day)
Order Handling per order		$4.75	$7.75	$14.75
Pick & Pack per Unit		$0.75	$0.75	$0.75
Weight Handling per lb.*	First 15 lb.	$0.45	$0.55	$1.50
	+ next 16-70lbs	$0.45	$0.70	$1.75
	More than 20lbs	See Oversize Media and Non-Media		

Example

Digital Camera sold using Multi-Channel Fulfillment

The example below is a guide in evaluating FBA only. Amazon does not warrant the accuracy of the calculations.

- Weight: 2 lb.
- Dimensions: 7" x 6" x 3" (.073 cu. ft.)
- Shipping method: Standard

Fee	Calculation	Amount
Order Handling	1 order x $4.75	$4.75
Pick & Pack	1 Unit x $0.75	$0.75
Weight Handling	3 lb* x $0.45	$1.35
Selling on Amazon Fees	N/A	
Total		$6.85

*Multi-Channel Fulfillment Weight Handling. Total shipment weight is calculated by adding a dunnage factor of 10 percent to the combined total of the individual Unit weight of each Unit in the shipment, then rounding up to the nearest pound.

You can calculate your Multi-Channel Fulfillment rates prior to sending inventory to FBA. You can also experiment with your FBA inventory by making 'pretend orders' and reviewing the rates for Standard (Ground), Expedited (2-Day Air), and Priority (Overnight) shipping services.

I just did a 'pretend order' in my Amazon seller account on a five pound item. Total fulfillment fees (includes picking, packing, boxes, shipping, etc.) are as follows:

Standard (Ground): $7.75

Expedited (2-Day Air): $11.25

Priority (Overnight): $23.00

This is for anywhere in the USA. It is not based on zip code; it is based on fixed fees and weight. Once these costs are known, you can then price your items strategically on other channels (more on this later). For comparison, here are the UPS Published Rates and Daily Rates for a five-pound shipment from Massachusetts to Washington State:

Ground Published: $13.98 – one week in transit

Ground Daily: $9.76 – one week in transit

2-Day Air Published: $44.25 – two days in transit

2-Day Air Daily: $35.04 – two days in transit

Overnight Published: $77.00 – one day in transit

Overnight Daily: $67.04 – one day in transit

Remember, in addition to being more expensive to ship it myself, I would also have to store the product, be home to process orders, keep boxes and other packing materials on hand, pick and pack my own orders, print shipping labels, and then get my boxes to UPS or the Post Office. Easy choice if you ask me!

Inbound Shipping Fees

To use Multi-Channel Fulfillment, you have to get your items sent to an FBA fulfillment center. They have to be labeled properly with special barcodes so that Amazon can properly identify your items. You are able to use Amazon's partnered UPS rates for inbound FBA shipments. These are the best rates around. Depending on where you are located and what fulfillment center your items are going to, this will be about $.20 – $.60 per pound.

Storage Fees

Amazon does charge storage fees based on unit volume. These rates are very low and can easily be managed by only sending in enough supply to match your sales volume. Many sellers find the storage rates to be so attractive that they want to send their entire inventory to FBA. It is recommended that you only send in a maximum of one year's supply at a time. Amazon does charge a Long term Storage Fee of $45/cubic foot for items left in FBA inventory more than one year. This fee does not apply to single units for each item so you can still send in Long Tail items (items that will sell, just not very often). Just only send in either one unit at a time for slow-moving, 'Long Tail' items, or a maximum of one year's supply.

<u>Removal Fees</u>

If you no longer want to have your inventory in Amazon's fulfillment centers, you can request to have your items returned to you or destroyed. You can have your items returned to you for $.50 per unit for regular items and $.60 per unit for oversize items (this includes shipping). If you want Amazon to simply remove and destroy your inventory items, the cost is $.15 for regular items and $.30 for oversize items.

"Aha!" Moment #2 – How to LEVERAGE Multi-Channel Fulfillment

Having access to Multi-Channel Fulfillment at Amazon rates is a very powerful thing. Imagine UPS came to your small, fledgling eBay business and said that you can now have Amazon's UPS rates for all of your shipping needs. Impossible? Does this sound too good to be true? You could lower your shipping costs drastically without having to be a big shipper? This is essentially what you get by using FBA's Multi-Channel Fulfillment. Your shipping costs have just decreased meaning that your overall margins have just increased. Your shipping and order fulfillment rates are now significantly lower than your competitors; use this to your advantage! Here's how:

There is more to a purchase than 'just the item'. There is more to a transaction than just price; even on commodity-type items where you and your competition sell the exact same item. Consider the ways to differentiate yourself as a seller on eBay: feedback, return policy, a well-designed listing page (or not), and shipping options/speed (among others). The shipping is where you can now trump your competition by offering your customers something that they simply cannot offer (at least not at the price that it costs you).

There are several strategies that you can use. Since your shipping rates are now lower than your competitors', you can beat them on price and still make the same profit per item. This is an 'apples to apples' comparison. You may now be able to sell at a price that is profitable for you, but not for them. This may cause them to stop selling a product and you will not have to compete against them anymore (and prices will rise). You can also set up barriers to entry to new competition who can't figure out how you are able to make a profit on your items since they don't know that you are using FBA Multi-Channel Fulfillment.

Another strategy to use would be to offer premium shipping such as 2-Day Air on your products at the same price that your competitor charges for Ground shipping. This makes it a 'rotten apples to fresh apples' comparison. You are both selling apples and for the same price, but you are able to offer the customer MORE than your competitor can. If a buyer on eBay is buying a commodity-type item and they can get it for $100 from you in two days or they can get it from your competition for $100 but will have to wait a week or more, who do you think will get the sale? You are able to maintain margins and take the lion's share of the sales by offering your customers more but not increasing your overhead. This will drive your competition crazy, as they will think that you are paying high shipping rates to ship 2-Day Air and must not be making any money. Let them think that all they want; just keep it your little secret.

How to Increase Margins with Multi-Channel Fulfillment

The previous examples are valid ways to use Multi-Channel Fulfillment, but personally, I don't recommend these strategies, especially for small sellers. You are able to capture more sales, but that also comes with more work. I prefer to increase margins and differentiate myself as a seller from my competition and not compete solely on price. What I'll show you below is how using Multi-Channel Fulfillment allows you to effectively market your items at higher prices, while keeping your overall fulfillment costs the same. This increase in margin goes directly towards your business' bottom line.

This book is in the recommended reading section at the end of this book:

How to Sell at Margins Higher Than Your Competitors

By Lawrence L. Steinmetz & William T. Brooks

It will change the way you see price, buyers, and your competition. It is worth every penny. I only wish I had read it before I started selling on eBay when I used to try to compete solely on price!

Above we talked about how you can use Multi-Channel Fulfillment to stop fighting in the 'apples to apples' comparison game. When you can change it to an 'apples to oranges' comparison, you can then market your oranges against your competitor's apples (even though the actual items that you both sell are the exact same). You can make your oranges more attractive for the same price and capture sales, but I prefer to position my oranges as a premium seller. I can offer the same commodity-type item as my competition, but with faster shipping and charge more for it. I can charge more because I am offering more (fast delivery options vs. slow delivery options). You will find customers that will see the difference and the added value that you provide with your oranges and they will pay you more for it. This is how you increase your margins on the same items that your competitors sell.

On eBay, you can also now add the Get It Fast option to your shipping settings. I recommend offering 2-Day Air shipping for free and factoring in your fulfillment costs into the price of your item. Then, just calculate the difference between Expedited (2-Day) and Priority (Overnight) and make that the upcharge for Overnight shipping (or round it to something nice and clean like $9.95). Again, these are options that your competition simply cannot offer at a competitive price. EBay makes these options available because they know some buyers want their items FAST and these buyers are willing to pay more to get their items fast. They even let you sort search results showing only items with the Get It Fast option, essentially making your competition disappear, regardless of their prices. You are able to charge more because you are offering more. Here are two images I made to promote my eBay listings. Feel free to use them if you like.

Check out this example with costs and fee breakdowns. Note the increased Return On Investment (or ROI). This is the key.

RIDGID 24V Battery	Comp Low	Comp High	Locomodem FBA
Sales Price	$97.50	$97.50	$119.95
eBay Final Value Fee	$8.78	$8.78	$10.90
Paypal Fees (est. 3%)	$2.93	$2.93	$3.60
Listing Fees	$0.50	$0.50	$2.00
Shipped UPS Ground	UPS Ground	UPS Ground	UPS 2-Day Air
3 lbs., Residential			
Shipping Costs	$9.52	$13.59	$10.15
Boxes, tape, supplies, etc	$0.50	$1.50	$0.00
Inbound FBA Shipping	$0.00	$0.00	$0.50
NET	$75.27	$70.20	$92.80
Cost (Hypothetical)	$50.00	$50.00	$50.00
Margin $	$25.27	$20.20	$42.80
Margin %	50.5%	40.4%	85.6%

$17.53 – $22.60 more on each transaction and 35.1% – 45.2% higher margins.

This isn't even an 'apples to apples' comparison! In addition to making more money per sale, I'm doing less work AND my customers get their items faster. But don't just take my word for it; run the numbers yourself.

It's all about the perceived value of what you are offering. 2-Day Air shipping is incredibly valuable, especially to a buyer who needs their items fast. It would normally cost $30-$40 for 2-Day Air shipping on that five pound item, but they get that value from you for less. This is what makes your items more attractive than your competitor's.

This is not a volume game; it's a margins game. Sellers who consistently make the most margins will thrive in the good times and survive in tough times. Sellers who ignore margin and try to 'make it up in volume' will work way too hard for too little of a reward. Always run the numbers!

Different channels may fare better by using different strategies. Learn the customer base of each one and market your items appropriately. What works on eBay may not be the best strategy for your own website. A combination of these strategies is also something to consider.

Limitations:

FBA Multi-Channel Fulfillment is currently only for domestic orders, although I would expect that Amazon is working towards adding more international options. If you get a lot of international orders, you may want to consider keeping some of your items on hand to ship yourself and only sending a portion of your inventory to Amazon's fulfillment centers.

(The fees included in the examples in this chapter were accurate at the time of writing. As with any service, fees may increase or decrease over time. Always check the most current fee schedules on Amazon.com and eBay.com).

Chapter 22 – So Why Isn't Everybody Doing This?

It's a fair question! When you understand how easy the principles of this business are, you may think that there must be so many people out there doing this that there's no room for you to join in all the fun. If you have this mentality then you need to snap out of it! The only people out there who want you to have this mindset are the people who are already doing this and fear competition. They know that there are so many easy deals out there and they want them all for themselves. They have a mentality of scarcity instead of one of abundance.

But you don't just have to take my word for it; you can grab your smartphone, get in your car, and go out and see if everything written in this book isn't 100% true. You can see for yourself if there are items in your area that you can buy locally and sell online for a profit.

You can also join any of the many online groups where sellers are actively helping each other and sharing their success stories. Need help? Just ask!

This business is fun and financially rewarding, but it is still a business and requires real work. Real work means that some people will not do this business even if they know how it works.

All of my friends and family know exactly what I do. Well, they sort of know what I do because trying to fully explain resale and FBA is not always the simplest conversation. They know that I go to stores and buy stuff to sell online. If they looked around my house they would probably think that I'm not a very big seller since I don't have a lot of inventory. That, of course, is the power of FBA. When I try to explain this business to them, it usually goes right over their heads.

Every now and then a friend or family member will ask me to teach them how to get started in this business. I'm happy to teach them, especially if they can pick up deals that I simply cannot. I'd rather someone that I know go get a deal and make some money than for it to sit there unclaimed or go to another seller that I don't know.

Some people are not comfortable with any kind of risk and that's OK. This business does have risks, but those risks are both small and manageable. When you understand the principles and dynamics of this business and use all of the information available to you, then this business is as close to a risk-free business model as I have ever seen.

Just having the knowledge presented in this book is simply not enough to make instant profits. A person has to take this knowledge and apply it. They have to go out and find items to resell. They have to make that first purchase. They have to prepare that first FBA shipment.

Even though people understand this business, not everyone takes action. Not everyone has the time to pursue the resale opportunities that they find. They say that they don't have the time but it's really just an excuse. They could find the time if they were serious about this business, but they may be too comfortable in their regular full-time job to see the opportunities in front of them.

Not everyone has the available funds with which to buy inventory. Knowing the information in this book is great, but if someone is unable to purchase any inventory for resale, then their business won't get very far. Some people may now possess this knowledge but find themselves living in a location with no signs of civilization (retail stores) or they may not even have a car in order to go to the stores.

If a new seller has a goal of $5,000 profit per month, every month, but they only have $500 with which to buy inventory, then they are setting themselves up to fail. You have to run the numbers! Set your goals and back out the numbers. Make these goals realistic and attainable so that you don't simply discourage yourself for any reason other than unrealistic expectations.

Take this simplified example: say you have a goal of making $5,000 per month in profit. If you sell items with 100% margin (meaning that you are doubling your money), then you have to be able to spend $5,000 per month. Is this something that you are comfortable with? Do you have $5,000/month to spend on inventory?

This needs to be run like a business. A $5,000 purchase is a big deal, but train yourself to look at it differently. This is your business spending $5,000 on inventory and not you personally spending $5,000. As sales come in, turn these profits around into more inventory. Keep it snowballing as your sales increase and your revenue grows.

Remember, even if another seller buys some inventory, they may not be able to purchase ALL OF IT. Some of the deal examples that I showed you in this book involved some pretty big numbers and not everyone will be either comfortable with purchases that large or financially able to make these large purchases. All this means is that there will never be a time when other sellers take all the opportunities. It's simply not possible. So even if someone else is doing this business, they are not doing it at a scale that in any way prevents you from finding plenty of deals in your area.

The lifestyle of a self-employed entrepreneur is great, but it's not for everyone. Many people like the reassurance of that static paycheck every two weeks. That steady paycheck also comes with steady hours and a steady schedule. This is probably the number one reason that people do not do this business. They are so used to something else that making any kind of switch from their regular routine is just too much of a change for them to make.

The business of resale, especially resale with FBA, is the perfect one to start because you can start small while you keep a full-time job. Are you willing to take the steps required to start building a profitable side business? Not everyone is. It is up to you to actually get started.

This side business can quickly grow into something big and lucrative. So big, in fact, that it may soon take over your regular job and make you 100% self-employed! Getting to this point means that you took lots of steps along the way. Unfortunately so many people never take these steps. No one has to take these steps; there's nothing wrong with a regular full-time job. But if you want to take control of your schedule and start capitalizing on the opportunities all around you by learning and applying the principles outlined in this book, then you have to actually get out there and do it! Some people won't and that is their choice. What is YOUR CHOICE? I can't make you get started; only you can do that. I can write chapter after chapter and book after book, but only you can take the steps toward building this business for yourself.

Basically, don't worry about everybody else. You'll only psych yourself out of this business, which is only good news for your competition.

Two Kinds of Critics

As you read this book and decide what kind of reseller you want to be, I encourage you to share and discuss this business model with friends and family. You may find someone who wants to partner up (which would be great, especially when you are first starting out) and you may find critics who say that this business is not possible.

Some critics will not believe this business model works even if you show them examples and payouts and bank accounts. There are plenty of naysayers out there.

Some critics KNOW that this is a powerful business model and will attempt to steer you the wrong way to prevent competition. You may run into another reseller who tries to sway you from continuing with your business when you run into them at a store or book sale. They'll say things like how there are no good books anymore and how they are probably going to stop doing this business because there is no money in it anymore. Boo-hoo. **If they actually believed what they said, would they be out scouting?**

You may find critics online who say that this business is dried up and that there are no opportunities out there anymore. They want you to believe them so that you get discouraged.

The theme of this book is EDUCATION. This business doesn't work because I say it works; it works because it actually works!

Understand the ins and outs of this business as well as the WHYs and HOWs and you'll be able to decide FOR YOURSELF if this business is legitimate or not. Don't listen to other people and don't just listen to me! Take what I write in this book and TEST IT FOR YOURSELF. Then decide what you're going to do.

Hard work and due diligence is rewarded.

Chapter 23 – Summary – Go Feed Your Amazon Monster!

Well there you have it. That's pretty much everything that I know about arbitrage, selling online, and FBA. I'm sure I could fill more pages with stories of running into grumpy booksellers and retail store adventures, but I have to stop writing at some point. ☺

Once you grasp the fundamentals of this business you'll see that it's a fairly simple process of scouting, listing, and selling. Then just repeat the process. You'll also see that this really isn't all that difficult. The business that you set up is almost like a machine that is on autopilot. This machine cranks out more if you put more into it. Work harder, it produces more. Work less, it produces less.

Since you do have to put dollars and products into this business machine that you've created, I like to refer to it as 'Feeding Your Amazon Machine', or to make it more memorable, 'Feeding Your Amazon Monster'. You have created a monster (the good kind) and you have to feed it. You wake up each day and what do you have to do? Feed your Amazon Monster! The more you feed it, the more it grows. You can even give it a name. That way when your friends and family ask you what you are up to, you can just tell them that you are feeding your monster; his name is Sparkles.

After you try to explain to them what you do, and they look at you like maybe you're the one whose name is Sparkles, just hand them this book. It will make your life much easier.

I truly believe that anyone can take the knowledge contained in this book and start a successful arbitrage business at whatever scale they are comfortable with. You can work extremely part time hours and make some extra supplemental income, or you can go full steam ahead and make this your full time (and very profitable) business. I've listed many sources for inventory as well as reasons why no one can possibly ever take over all of the deals out there in the bonus sections at the end of this book. There are likely many more sources and creative ways to find inventory that I have not even considered. Keep on thinking of new ways to run this business and you'll continue to learn and grow.

My final piece of advice is this; find trustworthy people, work with them, and stay with them. The hardest thing to find is people that you can trust. If you are working with people right now that you do not trust, then I would recommend that you re-evaluate those relationships. When you surround yourself with people that you can trust, then you are free to talk about ideas without fear of being undermined.

I read on message boards where people will not even tell their own friends and family about their online business. They are worried that they will learn the business, become a competitor, and put them out of business somehow. It's a shame that some people feel as though they cannot share this business model with friends or family because they fear that they will be inviting a ruthless competitor. If you are truly afraid of this happening, then you are hanging around people that you do not trust. This will severely limit how successful you can make this business or any other venture. Finding someone that you can work with and bounce ideas off of will help your business grow.

One of the biggest reasons that ScanPower works and has enjoyed great success is because of the level of trust enjoyed by everyone on the ScanPower team.

I wrote this in the Introduction and I'll write it here as well:

If you have any questions about this business, I invite you to call or email me directly.

214-298-6866 – yes, that is my cell phone number and I invite you to call (or send a text message if that's your thing). I'm Eastern Standard Time so please consider the time when calling. Also, please read the whole book before you call. ☺

If you prefer email: chris@scanpower.com

For general technical support for ScanPower, please visit the support & help pages at http://www.scanpower.com

Or send an email to support@scanpower.com and someone from the ScanPower support team will be happy to help.

I wish you nothing but great success in this exciting business. If there is anything that I can do to help, I'm just a phone call, text, or email away.

To your success,

Chris Green

Director, ScanPower.com

Facebook.com/chris

214-298-6866

When you are done reading this book, feel free to sell it back on Amazon using FBA!

You may be asking yourself, could that actually work? Is that possible?

Ask Jim Rice:

Jim Rice
I read in an earlier post where somebody sold their $9.95 copy of Retail Arbitrage on AZ for a much higher price. Since I also had one of those $9.95 copies I decided to give it a try. I think I under priced it at $80 because it was purchased immediately upon check-in. You must be doing something right Chris if your books are that popular :)

Unlike · Comment · Unfollow Post · September 5 at 10:39am

You and 3 others like this.

 Chris Green It's like an infinite loop of a glitch in the matrix or something when you can buy a book for $10 and that book tells you to sell itself for $80 and it works.
September 5 at 4:10pm · Like · 3

Thanks, Jim!

(posted in our ScanPower Facebook Group on September 5, 2012)

Shameless Plug – What is ScanPower?

ScanPower is the ONLY all in one solution for Amazon sellers with a focus on FBA.

ScanPower MOBILE

Let's starting with acquiring products to sell. ScanPower MOBILE for iPhone, iPad, and Android devices lets you scan any barcode and see what it's selling for on Amazon and how much money you can make by selling it. Whether you're doing Retail Arbitrage sourcing or placing wholesale orders at tradeshows, ScanPower MOBILE gets you the pricing data that you need FAST. ScanPower Mobile is also fully integrated with the entire suite of ScanPower products meaning you can scan once and create lists of products to upload to Amazon or even bulk evaluate. With ScanPower MOBILE, you'll make better buying decisions.

ScanPower Buy Button

What the Buy Button is designed to do is to allow you to 'SAVE' the items that you buy while out on a scouting trip. If you are buying books at a thrift store or toys at a retail store, you can build a list of the items that you plan to purchase. This Buy List can then be uploaded from ScanPower on your phone directly to ScanPower on your PC or Mac for fast and easy processing.

HotList Feature

This is an easily accessible list of pre-formatted links that allow you to quickly research items on other websites like Google or eBay.

Scan or search, the choice is yours!

ScanPower mobile is not only a barcode scanning app, but so much more. Can't find a barcode, no problem — search by keyword!

ScanPower WEBSCOUT

Doing Online Arbitrage or any kind of online sourcing? ScanPower WEBSCOUT is the web-based version of ScanPower MOBILE and is included with all ScanPower packages.

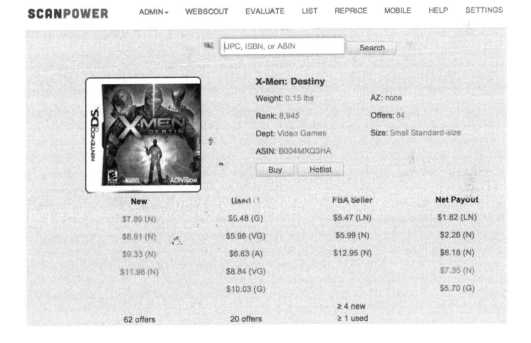

ScanPower EVALUATE

ScanPower EVALUATE is the professional Amazon seller's choice for bulk evaluation of potential inventory. Simply take a vendor list of UPCs and upload them to ScanPower EVALUATE. You'll be given a file with complete pricing information including Amazon's price, sales rank, FBA competition or lack thereof, number of sellers, lowest price, payout, and more. With ScanPower EVALUATE, you'll quickly be able to find the most profitable items from large lists of potential inventory.

ScanPower LIST

Once you have products to sell, you need to get them listed! ScanPower LIST is a **one-touch system** designed to quickly get your inventory listed, priced, and labeled for shipment to Amazon's warehouses. With ScanPower LIST, you scan an item, set condition, price, condition notes, and print the FBA label as you go. You then place it in the box to go to Amazon completing the entire process and only touching the item once. ScanPower LIST handles split shipments as you go so you always know where your inventory is headed. With ScanPower LIST, you'll list your inventory faster, saving you time and money.

ScanPower LIST is a web-based program for Mac or PC (Firefox or Chrome recommended). ScanPower LIST will synchronize with your existing inventory in order to replenish inventory or create new listings. Dymo Direct printer settings are built in so that you can print individual FBA labels on your Dymo label printer without the need to manually change your printer settings.

ScanPower REPRICER

Now that you have inventory in Amazon's warehouses, you have to keep it competitively priced. ScanPower REPRICER automates this process with pricing rules that you set and control to match your specific seller goals and pricing strategies. Want to be the lowest overall price? ScanPower REPRICER can do that. Want to be the 5th lowest FBA price? ScanPower REPRICER can do that, too. Set up multiple Rule Groups with one for Books & Media and another for Toys & Games. With ScanPower REPRICER, you are always in control.

Detailed, step-by-step walk through demonstrations are built into ScanPower REPRICER.

ScanPower Accounting

These features give users the ability to track virtually everything related to your FBA business.

▪ **Expense Tracking** - track your expenses by brand, source, MSKU, product type, etc.

▪ **Inventory Reports** - run inventory reports by product type, source, shipment, and more! You will also have the option to run aging reports.

▪ **Sales Reports** - calculate your return on investment (ROI) by source, brand, category, etc.

Sales Dashboard

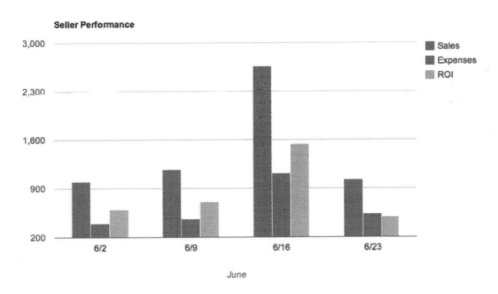

With a dedicated support team standing by, ScanPower helps sellers of all experience levels be successful on Amazon.

Give ScanPower a try and take your Amazon business to the next level.

Use referral code AMAZONBOOK to get an extended one-month trial of ScanPower as a special thanks for purchasing this book. New users can sign up here: scanpower.com/store

ScanPower WebScout — $9.95/mo

Web Source. Unlimited web-based scouting using our Mac & PC compatible WebScout program.

**WebScout is NOT a mobile app.

ScanPower Reprice — $25/mo

Reprice. Unlimited interactive repricing using our web-based repricing program (Mac & PC compatible).

ScanPower List — $39.95/mo

List. Unlimited ScanPower Listing using our 'one-touch' web-based listing program (Mac & PC compatible).

Web Source. Unlimited web-based scouting using our Mac & PC compatible WebScout program.

Reprice. Unlimited interactive repricing using our web-based repricing program (Mac & PC compatible).

ScanPower Mobile — $39.95/mo

Source. **Unlimited ScanPower Mobile Scouting on iPhone, iPad, or Android devices.

Web Source Unlimited web-based scouting using our Mac & PC compatible WebScout program.

ScanPower Pack — $59.95/mo

Source. **Unlimited ScanPower Mobile Scouting on iPhone, iPad, or Android devices.

Web Source Unlimited web-based scouting using our Mac & PC compatible WebScout program.

List. Unlimited ScanPower Listing using our one-touch web-based listing program (Mac & PC compatible).

Reprice. Unlimited interactive repricing using our web-based repricing program (Mac & PC compatible).

Bonus #1 – How to Compete Against Amazon

If you sell on Amazon long enough, you will run into Amazon as a competitor. This can be intimidating! Competing against Amazon is not something to take lightly. They are able to sell at margins and prices that they find acceptable but that most sellers would not. This can cause them to lower price to a level at which you may feel that you can no longer compete. They may even sell items at a loss. They also have advanced algorithms and monitoring tools in place behind the scenes that allow them to 'dial in' exactly what they want to sell the item for and how to position themselves against their competition.

It's Amazon's site and they make the rules. The best that you can do is to understand the rules and compete in the best way that you can.

Here are some strategies to effectively compete against Amazon.

Hold Price

Sometimes Amazon is selling at a price that you simply cannot match or even beat. When you find yourself in this position, sometimes it is best to just hold your price and see what happens. Amazon has been known to sell out of a product, both temporarily and permanently. When this happens, buyers will have to look to other sellers for the product. There is a big difference in an item being $49.95 and IN STOCK and being $49.95 and OUT OF STOCK. If Amazon is out of stock, then your $59.95 price might look pretty good.

Here's another scenario that can happen. Remember that price is set by supply and demand. Price is also only constant at one point in time. As time goes by and supply and demand change, so will price. Price may be low today but higher in the future (consider popular toys at Christmas time, seasonal products, or when Oprah recommends something). If your business model supports it, simply holding price and seeing how the market develops can be a strategy that pays off instead of instantly liquidating inventory at the first sign of Amazon competition.

Play the Up and Down Game

This can be fun. Amazon is bound by the same limitations of the physical world as the rest of us are. So even though they are monitoring prices and competitors on products that they sell, they cannot do it instantly. It takes a while for the computers to sync up, calculate changes and implement those changes. There are windows of opportunity that you can take advantage of if you know how the game is played. I learned this from experience. It cost me money the first time, but I learned the system, so it was tuition that I was more than willing to spend.

I was selling a cordless screwdriver with a market price of $19.95. I had fifty units and I received these for free as a bonus for purchasing a separate item that I was also selling. I labeled the items and sent them to FBA when Amazon was also selling the item. I priced mine at $18.95 to get the sale based on price. I sold some and then Amazon dropped to $18.95. As a buyer myself, I would choose to buy from Amazon over a third party seller so I dropped my price to $17.95. I got a few sales and then noticed that Amazon was now $17.95. We played this game until the price was $6.95! I was frustrated but since my cost was zero, I was taking it all in stride and trying to figure out how to play this game to my advantage. The first thing that I thought of was that I should buy up all of Amazon's stock at $6.95, label it and send it all back to FBA and be the only seller at $19.95. This could work, but it would be risky as Amazon could likely get more in stock from the manufacturer so this would leave only a small window of time where they were out of stock and I could get all the sales at full price.

At $6.95 I was not happy since I was really just giving them away. I only had a few units left, so I raised the price back up to $19.95 to prevent sales at the $6.95 price while I thought about what to do. You can probably already guess what happened next; Amazon raised their price to

$19.95! Lesson learned! Amazon will compete on prices GOING DOWN, but they will also stay competitive when prices GO UP! So we played our little game again when I cut price by $1 and got a few sales until Amazon caught up. These sales were at a profitable level (not down at a silly $6.95 price). Unfortunately, by now I had sold out of my fifty units and while I did make profit on the items, I didn't make as much as I could have if I had known how Amazon reacted to competition from the beginning. And what did Amazon do when I sold out? They raised price back to $19.95.

Creating New, Custom Bundled Products

The next bonus chapter outlines how to create new product pages on Amazon and why doing so can be quite profitable. There is also a strategy to compete against Amazon that involved not only creating these new product pages, but creating new 'bundles' of products that are already listed on Amazon.

As an Amazon seller with a Sell Professionally account, you can create new product pages (doing so often requires a UPC and where to get a UPC is listed in the next bonus chapter). So you can take a product that is selling well and then bundle it with a complimentary product in order to provide convenience and value to the customer. **You now have a brand new Amazon product page with no competition!**

You can also create new product pages that consist of a multi-pack of an item that a buyer may want multiple quantity of. This is also a good strategy from a seller's perspective because the fee structure will show you that you will make more per item selling a 12-pack of something to one buyer than selling 12 individual items to 12 customers.

When creating new product bundles, just be sure to follow the Amazon guidelines for bundled products:

http://www.amazon.com/gp/help/customer/display.html?nodeId=200442390

Bundles: General Policy

Well-designed product bundles provide convenience and value to buyers. Adhering to this policy, including the below guidelines for the creation of bundles, will help Amazon.com customers locate specific bundles more easily, and prevent duplicate or near-duplicate listings.

Sellers can create bundles composed of different products to create a new bundled product. Bundled products may be listed in all categories except Books, Music, Video, and DVD (collectively, BMVD) and Video Games. Bundles are only allowed when the primary product in the bundle is not a BMVD or Video Games product. For example, you can list a bundle composed of a yoga mat (the primary product), a yoga DVD and a yoga book, but you cannot list a bundle composed of a yoga DVD and a yoga book.

The referral fee applicable to the product category in which the bundle is listed will apply to the entire bundle.

Use Multi-Channel Fulfillment

As mentioned in Chapter 20, you can use Multi-Channel Fulfillment to fulfill orders from any number of other sales channels such as eBay. Not all buyers buy from Amazon, even if they have the best price. Some buyers still think that Amazon only sells books and some buyers simply don't like Amazon and want to spend their money elsewhere. The market price on Amazon.com can be unprofitable for you but don't let this stop you from listing and selling on other channels where the market price is still at a profitable level. The online markets are not efficient; Amazon may sell an item for $100 that sells on eBay for $150 or vice versa. Sell your items on the sales channel where it makes the most sense and remember that the Amazon price is set by the Amazon supply and demand. Those are both only pieces of the overall supply and demand.

Another thing to remember is that even when Amazon sells an item, they face some of the same limitations that all sellers face. That includes possibly selling out of a popular item. When Amazon sells an item and then they sell out, the secondary market takes over. Odds are, if Amazon has sold out, that the item is popular and the market price is too low. Price on the secondary market will rise in situations like this when demand outpaces supply. Sometimes you can predict when this will happen. A good strategy for this is to raise your price in order to not compete with Amazon while Amazon has the item in stock in anticipation of Amazon selling out.

In the event that having Amazon as a competitor no longer makes the item profitable to sell, sometimes it is best to get out and just move on. There are so many opportunities out there to take advantage of, so don't get caught up on one product. Stay smart and watch your margins.

Bonus #2 – Creating New Product Pages for Items NOT on Amazon

When you are buying items to sell on Amazon through FBA, ScanPower will give you the complete pricing picture so that you can make the best buying decisions and lower your risk. But sometimes you will find an item that ScanPower shows is not in the Amazon catalog at all. So now what do you do? You have less information with which to make a buying decision. Less information means higher risks, but higher risks can also mean higher rewards.

You may find an item that shows no match in the Amazon catalog, but it's an item that you've seen on national TV. Or maybe it's a different version of a product that already exists and is selling well on Amazon. Or it's a store exclusive of a strong brand like 'Toys R Us Exclusive' Barbie doll or an 'Only At Target' Disney Cars Giftset. Consider as many pieces of information that you can and then make a decision to either purchase the item in order to create a new product page on Amazon or to move on. If you find yourself thinking too hard about an item, I recommend moving on. There are too many good deals out there to worry too much about a single item. If the item is intriguing, think about it later. It will still be there tomorrow. Don't slow yourself down and miss other opportunities because of indecisiveness.

Knowing if an item is sold on Amazon or not is a powerful piece of information in itself. You now know that if you were to list this item on Amazon, that you would be the only seller. As the only seller, you would be the one who sets price since you would not have other sellers to compete with. When you set price, remember that people put different values on items. Some buyers will value an item at $50 that other buyers only value at $10. When you control the entire supply available on Amazon, you can market your items to the Amazon buyers who place the highest value on the item. Remember, it's not about volume; it's about margin.

Over time, if the item is bringing you good profits, the odds are that another seller will find this same opportunity. As competition enters the market, prices will change. Keep selling the item as long as you are making profit margins that are acceptable to your business model. If an item attracts too much competition and the price falls to a level that is not profitable, simply stop selling the product. That is one of the best things about arbitrage; you're never tied to a product long term. You have complete control and you can react quickly to any sudden market changes.

To make a new listing for an item that shows no match for the UPC, first do a title search on Amazon.com for the product. There are times where the product exists on Amazon but it is simply not tied to the UPC. If you do find a product page for the item, look it over very carefully to be sure that it is an exact match (or not). Some products vary only slightly and those slight differences can be very important.

If the product does not exist, then you can start the process on Amazon of creating a new product. You'll be asked to enter the UPC for the item as you create it.

If you want to create a product page for a product that does not have a UPC, then you'll have to buy a UPC. When I first started selling on Amazon, I had no idea that you could buy a UPC, but as soon I learned this little trick, it was off to the races! Creating Amazon product pages out of thin air for any product that you wanted to sell is an amazingly powerful thing to do. I would do this for special power tools that were only available as part of a combo kit at retail stores. If a buyer wanted to buy this particular tool, they could buy the $500 combo kit and pay for a bunch of stuff that they don't really need, or they could buy it from me for $100 on Amazon. Did I sell to everyone who wanted this tool? No, but I sold it to the buyers who valued it at $100.

Here are a couple of sites that sell single UPCs. You get a price break if you buy in bulk:

http://www.cheap-upc-barcode.com/

http://www.singleupc.com/

http://www.qualityupc.com/

You can also search online for many other websites that sell UPCs. They are also sold on eBay of all places.

Like we mentioned earlier, other Amazon sellers can piggyback on your newly created listings. There is not a whole lot that you can do about it if they are selling the exact same product that you are selling. Amazon is not eBay, where each seller makes his or her own page for each product. Amazon is one page per product and all sellers list their price and descriptions on this one page.

(This following bundling strategy (as well as the Amazon guidelines) was covered in the previous bonus chapter as a way to compete against Amazon, but it is also a strategy for simply creating new pages and selling new products).

What you can do is make it difficult for other sellers to match your newly created product pages exactly. If other sellers are not offering the EXACT same item, Amazon will stop them from listing on the product page. There are a few ways to do this. One way is to bundle a low cost item with your original item. You may be selling a poker chip set but you also bundle in a special low cost card protector. For another seller to list on your product page, they would have to be able to acquire and bundle the exact same card protector.

You can also create new product pages for custom bundles of complimentary products. Skip McGrath of http://www.skipmcgrath.com has had great success with this method. He was selling knife sets and cutting boards separately but the competition was forcing prices down to non-profitable levels. Rather than give up on the products, he bundled them together under a newly purchased UPC and sold his bundles for more than if a buyer purchased the items separately. You may already be thinking, "Why would a buyer do this?" It's been a theme throughout this book that FBA sellers enjoy a premium position in the Amazon marketplace as well as how buyers do not always compare every possible option when making buying decisions. A buyer sees Skip's bundle, likes the price, buys it, and gets on with their life. This happens every day on Amazon.

Skip has also had great success with working with companies to sell their products online and give Skip the 'Amazon Exclusive'. This type of agreement means that Skip will be the only one that the company allows to sell their products online on Amazon.com. This type of agreement can help you maintain margins on Amazon by blocking potential competitors. This is good for you as a seller and it is also good for the company who may not want their product or brand to be watered down by sellers who drive price down unnecessarily. If you are able to set up some Amazon exclusive product lines, you can enjoy a nice profit while not always being concerned about price and competition.

Things to look for to find potential 'Amazon Exclusive' items:

Not Currently on Amazon

This is key of course. Like we talked about earlier in this book, Amazon customers want to buy from Amazon as their preferred place to shop. As more and more products become available, more and more customers will be able to do a larger percentage of their overall shopping online.

Small Companies

Small companies who do not sell on Amazon or do not sell online at all are good to approach for Amazon exclusive agreements. They will be more receptive to new and innovative ways to get their brand or products distributed to consumers. As with any agreements that you enter into, be sure to make a win-win type of situation.

Destination-type Products

A product that is a destination product means that buyers will want it regardless of price. The buyer needs the product or wants the product and this need or want is greater than their desire to get the product at a low price or discount.

Grocery & Gourmet Food products can be good destination products because people who use them may put an above-average preference on a particular item and this personal preference can override price sensitivity in the buying decision process.

Creating new products or new custom bundles is a great way to carve out your own niche on Amazon. If you have special knowledge about a product or groups of products, you can make new product pages for items that are attractive to buyers. If these are things that your competition cannot match exactly, then you'll have your own set of listings on which you will enjoy exclusivity.

Here's one more trick about creating new listings. More importantly, this is how to gauge which items warrant creating a new listing. When you see reviews online or in magazines for new products or Top Ten Lists for certain products, you can bet that there are many people who will see and read these articles. Consider products reviewed by Consumer Reports magazine or featured on Yahoo.com. These magazines and websites have readerships in the millions. When they make a Top Ten List for their readers that feature products like the top ten curling irons under $50, you can bet that there is a sub-group of those readers out of the entire group of readers who will want to purchase that number one rated product. Out of that sub-group of readers who want to purchase that product, there is a sub-group of readers who want to purchase that product online. Out of that sub-group of readers who want to purchase that product and want to purchase that product online, there is a sub-group of readers who want to purchase that product from Amazon.com. Out of that sub-group of readers who want to purchase that product, want to purchase that product online, and want to purchase that product from Amazon.com, there is a sub-group of readers who want to buy from Amazon directly or from an FBA seller because of preference, trust, FSSS (Free Super Saver Shipping) or Prime shipping options. Out of that sub-group of readers who want to purchase that product, want to purchase that product online, want to purchase that product from Amazon.com, and want to purchase from Amazon directly or from an FBA seller, there is a sub-group that will value the product at different levels. Some will want to buy the product for the listed price, some will only want the product if they can get it at a discount, and some will buy the product regardless of price because they want that number one rated curling iron regardless of price. They see something in a magazine or on a website and they have to have it from Amazon or an FBA seller. Those are the buyers that you can reach that your competition cannot.

When you see these articles and lists, check to see if the products are listed for sale on Amazon or not. If not, you may have just stumbled upon a new opportunity. I can pretty much guarantee that when articles like this run, it creates demand for the specific products on Amazon.com. If there is no supply, then the demand doesn't go away, it just doesn't enter into a transaction. If you can spot trends like this, and you can identify a source for the supply (either from the manufacturer or sourced at local retailers) you can be the seller who brings the supply to Amazon and is able to capture this demand at high margins.

Bonus #3 – Why No One Can Take Over

The thought may have crossed your mind. You may run into another reseller when you are out and about, scouting for products to sell. You may think that someone already has your neck of the woods 'covered' and that they are already getting all of the good deals. Let me tell you that the scenario of you running into another online seller may be real, but the scenario that they are able to scoop up all of the available deals simply is not possible.

There are a few restrictions in place that affect every online seller. They are the limited number of hours in a day, the amount of money that they can spend on inventory, and their physical capacity to transport products. Not to mention the sheer impossibility of being able to scan every item at every store. Some stores carry hundreds of thousands of different products. Calculate the time to scan each one and you start to see the scale of what we are talking about.

Hours in a Day

There are only 24 hours in a day and there arc only so many hours that some stores are even open. Online sellers can only be at one place at one time.

Disposable Income to Invest in Inventory

Some online sellers will have more disposable income with which to buy sellable inventory than others. Those sellers with less to spend on inventory will want to spend that money on the BEST products to sell online. There are varying degrees of deals to be found. Some items are good, but some items are great! Sellers with excess funds will have the option to buy both good and great deals and buyers with limited funds should focus on only the best deals. Both business models are profitable.

Capacity to Transport Products

I've run into this one several times. I'll find so many good products that they simply will not all fit in my vehicle to transport them home. I'll fill up five carts at Toys R Us and then have to re-evaluate the items and only purchase the great ones. The good ones have to go back for another trip or another day.

Different Target Margins

Similar to disposable income and transport capacity, having different target margins has to deal with how a seller chooses to run their business. When you compare the return on your money using arbitrage compared to what the bank gives you, it's easy to see why people start to get excited about this business. Some sellers will be happy making a 50% return on their money and some sellers will only want items that give a 300% return. Both are profitable and it is up to each seller to decide how they want to run their individual businesses.

A competitor who only buys the highest margin items will be leaving behind plenty of good items for other sellers.

Different Risk Tolerances

Different sellers will have different tolerances for risk. Some will take more chances on items that may not be fast sellers but have sky-high margins and some sellers may only want items that they feel will sell through in less than 30 days. Some will be willing to take chances on new products that are not in the Amazon catalog and therefore have less information regarding previous sales and competition. Each seller decides how they want to run their business and some will make riskier moves than others. Risk should not be seen as a bad thing; big risks often lead to big rewards. It is important to analyze all available information and only take calculated risks that you are comfortable taking.

Because of these different risk tolerances, different sellers will purchase different items for their resale businesses, even if out shopping side-by-side.

Different Knowledge

Different sellers will have different knowledge about different stores and products. Some will have a previous background giving them an advantage in certain categories and some will have been selling online for a long time and have gained experience over the years. Some will be brand new and will miss easy deals due to their lack of knowledge. This dynamic will always be changing and it is important for you to keep on learning and gaining experience.

Right Place, Right Time

This will happen to you at some point. You'll be in a store just as they are marking down items for clearance pricing. Or you'll look up in the overhead and spot a stack of toys that has been sold out everywhere and is a hot item. No one seller can be everywhere all the time. Don't psych yourself out and take yourself out of the game and think that this won't happen to you. Keep on scouting and keep your eyes open for deals and look for opportunities and you'll have plenty of success stories to tell your friends.

You will run out of time in each day or you will run out of money to spend before you run out of places to source products.

We've shared this statement online and people quickly agree that the only reasons they have to stop sourcing is that the day is over or they have spent all of their inventory funds.

Bonus #4 – The ZERO RISK Way to Start

Don't worry if a lot of this is going over your head. This is pretty high-tech, cutting-edge stuff. The business described here is one that was simply not previously possible in such a low-risk, efficient manner in which it exists today.

Running an arbitrage business this way is new and exciting and it can be difficult to explain. We're talking about a lot of new technologies and market dynamics that might not always make sense. LEARN as much as you can and when you don't understand something, ASK! There are many online groups that are more than happy to help new sellers 'get over the hump' of getting started.

If you are on Facebook, we have a Discussion Group here:

http://www.facebook.com/groups/scanpower/

Once you have all of your questions answered, you may still be wondering what to buy to resell. That's OK, it's normal to be cautious when just starting out. You are actually laying out your hard-earned cash for inventory. Here is how to start RISK FREE.

Get the free trial of ScanPower for iPhone or Android. If you use up your free trial and you're still not ready to subscribe to the service, use the Amazon app, Amazon Price Check, or Amazon Flow. Other apps are not as comprehensive, but they are better than nothing.

As you scan items and compare your costs to the Amazon market prices, you'll find some items with healthy margins. When you find something that you have confidence in, BUY IT. Use your credit card and KEEP YOUR RECEIPT. Take it home and list it on Amazon as Merchant Fulfilled (not FBA). Set your price where you are happy with the profit after all fees. Now sit back and wait.

One of two things will happen, both of which will not cost you money. You'll either get sales, which means you have to ship your orders out yourself as they come in. Or you won't get any sales. Getting sales means PROFIT in your pocket. If you don't get sales, and your confidence in the product goes down, simply delist your items and RETURN the product to the store with your receipt. Be sure to follow the store's return policy. Most stores will give you at least thirty days and I've never heard of a store having an issue with new items being returned in new condition with the receipt. Your refund will go straight to your credit card and even out your balance. This method is truly ZERO RISK. You either make money, or you are right back where you started with a little extra knowledge in your head, but either way you did not lose a penny.

There are some downsides to this model. You would have to be home to process and ship your own orders. You would have to go to the Post Office or find a UPS drop off location. You would not get the boost that FBA sellers see because your items would not be eligible for Amazon's free shipping programs like Free Super Saver Shipping and Amazon Prime.

Personally, I don't recommend making a habit of this (returning product to the stores). I outline it here as a proof-of-concept in order to truly get started without any monetary risk.

Bonus #5 – The Pixar Effect

Pretty much everyone knows Pixar. Pixar has brought us movies such as Toy Story, Cars, and Finding Nemo among others. Each of their movies has been wildly popular and when a movie is popular, the merchandise that goes with it is popular as well.

What is interesting about Pixar movies is how they stand the test of time. Pixar movies have spanned generations (and will continue to do so). Never in the history of entertainment have movies remained so popular for so long. In 2011, kids are still watching Toy Story for the first time. Toy Story came out in 1995! Name one other kid's movie that is popular the same way as Toy Story is sixteen years after its release. If you grew up in 1988, were you turning off Transformers and G.I. Joe to watch movies from 1972? In 1995, when Toy Story came out, are you still watching movies from 1979? Not likely. This is newly charted territory.

So what happens when a movie stands the test of time and its popularity spans generations? The merchandise stays popular long after the retail stores stop carrying it and move on to the next big thing.

There are a few reasons for this. The first is that they are just great movies. Kids and adults both enjoy watching Pixar movies. Another reason is the unprecedented access to various forms of media. People now have a near infinite amount of entertainment choices. With the Internet and services like TiVo and Netflix, people have access to practically every movie ever made at any time.

Having access to such a wide variety of media means that people can now discover shows that they would never have realized existed before. Have you ever heard of Pingu the Penguin or Oswald the Octopus? Me neither, until Netflix 'recommended' them because of the other shows that my kids watch on the computer. Now that kids can discover and watch shows that would normally be considered obscure at best, and for all practical purposes, non-existent, it creates a demand for the toys and related merchandise. This newly found demand would never be able to find the supply without the Internet. Prices for these toys, which can only be found on the secondary market, are sky high. But guess what? Some parents are willing to pay them. Remember, price is set by supply and demand. Supply may be small, and demand may be small, but some of the buyers that make up that demand have a much higher personal perceived value for the items. They are willing to pay higher prices for the items in short supply and the sellers are more than happy to sell to them at these prices.

Now consider this; someone whose first trip to the movies is to see Toy Story 3 can come home and delve into the entire history of Pixar movies instantly. Kids are not limited to what is on live television or what is available to rent at the local video rental store anymore. As they watch Finding Nemo, they tell their parents that they want some Finding Nemo plush toys, but they are not available in the stores anymore. These dynamics create a lingering strong demand for Pixar brand toys on the secondary market. Pair this DEMAND with sellers being able to make their SUPPLY known by listing online, and these toys are exchanged on the secondary marketplace at prices that both sides are happy with. This continues long after the movies have left the theaters.

Remember that Toy Story came out in 1995, A Bug's Life in 1998, Monsters, Inc. in 2001 and Finding Nemo in 2003. You can still find some Pixar brand merchandise from these movies in the stores today! Kids today are just as fascinated with a movie that came out back in 2003 as they are with the newest releases, but retail stores can't carry EVERYTHING that kids want because of physical limitations.

People are not limited to just what toys are on the shelf at the local store since they can now go online and find practically anything that their heart desires. Kids used to be limited to just what was available at the local toy store. Then you had mail order catalogs, and now you have Amazon.com.

Just a few generations ago, old store stock of toys from ten years ago would not have much value. Even those collectors (DEMAND) who did put a high value on the items (SUPPLY) had limited ways to find the items and complete the transaction. In today's marketplace with the Internet, eBay, Amazon, Craigslist and other sites, supply meets demand and buyers and sellers of even the most obscure items can transact business.

There is also the incredibly valuable branding of Pixar movies and characters. Pixar brand items can command a huge premium over identical, non-branded items. This goes for sippy-cups, bed sheets, pool toys, etc. The exact same item, but you pay more for the Pixar ones. Why? Because parents are willing to pay more to get their kids what they want.

Want proof? I sold Lightning McQueen Boo-Boo Buddies for $19.95 on Amazon.com through FBA. Non Lightning McQueen Boo-Boo Buddies sell for around $7. Almost three times the price premium for Lightning McQueen. I can also give you proof as parent and a buyer. One car from the Cars movie retails for almost $4. How about a regular Hot Wheels car? About $1. I'll give you one guess which one my little boy prefers and which one we end up buying. Yup, Lightning McQueen.

All of this is a fairly recent phenomenon and will extend well beyond Pixar. Understanding why this works will help you to stay ahead of your competition and recognize opportunities that your competitors will miss. It will also help you price your items properly to maximize your margins.

Bonus #6 – Attitude is Everything

I don't believe in karma, but I do believe that people will treat you the way that you treat them. If you're nice to people, they'll be nice right back to you. If you are rude, then don't expect much in return. This is a valuable chapter because in this business you will interact with other people. How you interact with them can determine your success level in this business.

When you are at a retail store, you will cross paths with store employees. If you are scanning barcodes and your little Scanfob® 2002 keeps going beep, beep, beep, they may ask you what you are doing. I always tell people to explain exactly what they are doing. Tell them that you are comparing online pricing information because you want to buy products to sell online. Store employees want to sell you things; that's what retail stores do, SELL THINGS. You tell them that you buy things, and many times they will try to sell you things. They just need to know what you want to buy. If you tell them that you like clearance items, they may lead you to a previously undiscovered aisle of clearance items.

If a store manager sees you buying a large amount of items, they may ask you what you are doing out of curiosity. They will be happy to see so many items being purchased. After all, they are running a retail store. You can often use this as an opportunity to explain what you do and ask for a discount. Make them an offer such as if you buy $1,000 will they take off 10%? Or if you fill up three shopping carts will they give you 25% off? Can't hurt to ask and they just might take you up on it. If you give them the cold shoulder and act paranoid and secretive, do you really think that they will go out of their way to offer you a discount? Me neither.

You may run into store employees or managers who are concerned about what you are doing. After all, they may have never seen someone come in and just start scanning all kinds of barcodes in their store before. They may think that you are price shopping for a competitor. It's their store and it's OK for them to ask what you are doing. This is where being honest and truthful counts. When you tell them what you are doing, it is very likely that they will be more than happy to just let you shop.

There may be rare times when a manager asks you to leave and you'll have to gauge the situation on a case-by-case basis. If the situation looks like it's not going to be resolved, just leave and find another store. You may want to return to the store another time and talk to the store manager one on one so that they truly understand what you are doing and you can answer any questions for them. Again, niceness goes a long way. Remind them that they want to sell things and that you want to buy things. Hopefully everyone is able to work it out.

When it comes to books at book sales and thrift stores, being nice goes incredibly far. If you are polite, look people in the eye, leave the books just as neat as when you found them, and buy a bunch of books, then you'll make friends at the book sale. They know that people come in and buy books to sell online. You may find the odd person who takes offense at this practice but the majority will see you as a book buyer and them as a bookseller. You should be good friends.

When you have a positive attitude, good things just seem to keep happening. If you grumble about, talk down to people, and make a huge mess out of the book stacks as you scan, do you really think that the people working at the book sale are going to go out of their way to help you? But if you are nice and courteous, don't be surprised when they pull out fresh boxes of books from the back and give you first shot at them. They may even cut you a deal on your books when you check out.

At thrift stores, books are often not very good sellers. If you come in and buy a cart full of books, their eyes will light up! That cart full of books is not only money in their register, but also books OUT OF THEIR STORE. Thrift stores want stuff selling so that they can put out more stuff. If you are buying stuff, they will like you.

I've told many, many thrift store employees exactly what I do. I haven't found one yet that has turned into a competitor. I find buying used books and selling them online through FBA to be not only profitable, but also fun! Not everyone does though. Make no mistake, this is a business and it is work. It also requires a commitment and some expensive equipment to start (although the startup costs for this business are pennies when you consider the income potential). More often than not, I'll explain what I do and chat with them for a little bit. They are more curious than anything. Many times they have offered to go in the back and bring out some more books for me to go through. Why? They want me to buy more books! Do you think they would offer to do this if I acted like I was too good to talk to them? Or simply ignored their questions? Not a chance.

Being nice pays off in this business as it does in life. I am not suggesting that you fake being nice to advance in this business. Life is too short for that. Be nice, be happy, and be positive. Life is too short and books are too plentiful to worry about a world of scarcity and be in a bad mood all day.

Not entirely related, but I always recommend giving an additional donation to the library sale when you check out. I usually try to round up around $20 so if my total was $181, I'd write them a check for $200. Running a book sale is a lot of hard work! It's not a ton of money, but every little bit helps and it's going to a good cause.

Bonus #7 – Your Lazy Competition

Oh how I love my competition! I know that they are out there even though I don't run into them very often. I see the scrunched up stickers that used to cover the UPCs on books that are pushed out of the way just enough to scan the barcode. I know that they have been there before although I'm never sure exactly when. I do know that I always find a ton of good stuff when I go out. I really can't remember ever leaving a store without buying something to sell online.

So, am I just getting lucky? Is there just always fresh stock when I'm at the stores? Not likely, I'm just not lazy. The number one thing that causes sellers to not make as much money as they could in this business is being lazy. They want it all to be easy. If it's not easy, they won't do it. I can see the allure of liking things easy, but the work that they are trying to avoid is not that hard! I think it's great that they are lazy. Your job is to not be lazy.

So what do they do that is lazy? Well, several things and these are all things that mean that they miss good books. This is good news for anyone who is not lazy and that's what I'm trying to teach you here.

One thing that they don't do is manually enter ISBNs. ISBN stands for International Standard Book Number and it is the 10 or 13 digit number that is often found above the UPC on a book. Some older books have no UPC on the back and they just have the ISBN. If not on the back, then it will be on the back of the title page. Books published prior to 1970 do not have ISBN numbers. Manually entering a 10-digit number into FBAScout is not hard (actually I use the voice recognition feature on Android. I get weird looks sometimes but that's OK), but I suppose it's harder than just scanning a barcode. So since lazy scanners don't enter ISBNs, there are always lots of good books left behind for me to scoop up with a few manual ISBN searches. Manual entry is simply not that hard and because so many of your competitors just don't do it, it means that you'll always be able to find good stuff.

Book sales are a place where my lazy competition really baffles me (but trust me, I don't mind at all). So many times at a book sale, my competition will hit it hard at the beginning and then after about two hours, 90% of them will leave the building. I read it online all the time where book sellers will say that there is no point in being at a book sale after the first two hours because all the scanners will have taken all the good books by then. I don't find this to be plausible. It's simply not possible due to the size of some book sales and the behavior of some scanners. Run the numbers on how many items are at the sale, how many items you can physically scan per hour and how many other scanners are at the sale. I think you'll find that the idea of everything being scanned and checked is pretty preposterous.

You'll see so many scanners picking and choosing books with UPCs to scan and never once entering an ISBN. They don't even scan every UPC in a section; they only selectively scan UPCs. If one scanner goes over one section then all other scanners assume that all of the good books in that section will have been taken. I really don't know why they think that. That scanner may only buy items with a sales price of $20+ and a Sales Rank of under 500K. This would leave a TON of good stuff left behind.

Also keep in mind that not everyone uses ScanPower. If they use an inferior service that does not provide accurate information, they will make poor buying decisions. They will make both kinds of poor buying decisions; buying books that will prove to be unprofitable as well as passing on books that are profitable.

Also remember that different sellers have different business goals. They may have a more limited amount of funds with which to invest in inventory and will therefore be more selective in the books that they buy. They also may not use FBA which would mean that they are dealing with space restrictions in terms of how many books they can physically add to their inventory as well as time limitations for listing new items and processing their orders. As an FBA seller, you have neither of these restrictions so your profit targets will be much, much different.

Remember, don't be lazy!

Bonus #8 – How To Run An FBA Consignment Business

You'll soon find that there is absolutely no shortage of things to sell online or buyers waiting to buy them. You may start to talk to and network with people who already sell online but maybe not on Amazon or maybe they sell on Amazon but they don't yet use FBA.

Once you are selling on Amazon using FBA, you will soon realize that you have no scaling restrictions anymore. You can grow as big as you're willing to grow; you just need more things to sell.

One thing to consider is running a consignment business. A consignment business is fairly straightforward. You partner with someone who has things to sell but who doesn't want to do the selling themselves. You, in exchange for doing the actual selling of the item, get a percentage of the proceeds. It's a win-win situation. The consignee is able to sell items and get paid, and you, the consignor, get more items to sell and earn a return for your time and effort.

Running a consignment business without FBA would be labor intensive in respect to the commitment in both time and storage. You could fill up your garage, your home, your shop, or a warehouse with other people's stuff to sell. If you have to ship all of the orders yourself, you will quickly be tied down to this business. Personally, this is not what I would want to do when FBA is out there waiting for me with open arms. ☺

As long as the products that you are selling on consignment have Amazon product pages, then you can list them on Amazon and use FBA for the entire process. What you need to know is how to keep track of whose inventory is whose when you are only using one Amazon account to sell items belonging to multiple people. The way to do this is with an identifier in your SKU prefixes.

Here is an Example:

Say you are selling books on consignment for an ex-college professor that you know named Mr. Ted. You would assign SKU numbers to their books beginning with TED. Simple enough, right? Then, when you get your detailed payout report from Amazon, you can sort the entire report by SKU number. This will group all of the TED SKUs together in one block. Copy and paste this block of SKUs into another Excel file where you can add up the totals for Mr. Ted's sales. You can then calculate their individual payout based on whatever terms you agreed upon.

We did consignment with our local library when we lived in Texas. Our agreement was 50% of the net payout (meaning ½ of the total that we received from Amazon after all Amazon and FBA fees). Their portion of the payout averaged about $10-$15 per book that was sold through our consignment agreement. They were very happy with the program as they were previously getting only $1 per book at their book sale. They dramatically increased their profit per book while doing no additional labor themselves. Win for them. Win for us because we were able to locate an additional source of sellable inventory.

When you use FBA to run a consignment business, there are really no limits to what you can do if you use your imagination and get a little creative.

I've read online about people who get upset when they find out that a bookseller has partnered with a local library to help them sell their books online. They get mad that one of their sources is gone and how dare that bookseller do something like that.

My response to them would be that there is absolutely nothing stopping them from doing the EXACT SAME THING. They could just as easily have talked to that library about partnering with them to sell their books online. They say they are upset that their source may be gone but I think they are actually upset at themselves for not working with the library and are misdirecting their frustration. Maybe I'm wrong; remember I majored in economics, not psychology.

Consignment with your local library is not the only thing you can do. How about consignment with your local thrift stores? Remember, when you are an FBA seller you have no space constraints so you can handle huge amounts of inventory. Just get it processed and sent to FBA. You could run a consignment business for every thrift store in your area. Don't get mad if you hear someone else is doing it because there is nothing stopping you from doing it yourself!

It's a difference in how you see the world around you. Do you see it as a land of scarcity? Or do you see it as a land of opportunity and abundance? I know the way that I see it!

Downsides to FBA Consignment Businesses

There are downsides to an FBA consignment business. It can be a lot to keep track of, especially if you have multiple consignees. You'll be responsible for monitoring their inventory items on FBA, calculating fees, avoiding Long Term Storage Fees, and all of the other details of selling on Amazon.com.

As I mentioned earlier in the book, there are downsides to FBA and those downsides apply here as well. Amazon or UPS may lose or damage your inventory. You may want to consider some additional types of business insurance to protect you and your consignees. You are also at the mercy of Amazon customer service for returns. A customer may return an item to you long after you have paid out your consignee for the item. Amazon will then debit your account for the purchase price leaving you in negative territory and you still have the item in unknown condition. Do you ask for a return of the consignee's payment? Or do you debit their next payout? There are different ways to do it, but be sure to consider these possibilities before entering into an agreement with someone.

These are all things to take into consideration when you decide if an FBA consignment business is the right thing for you. You may decide that buying inventory from people at a discounted price is a better strategy. They get paid instantly instead of slowly over time and you get the items at a discount but they are now solely your responsibility to sell. You do the selling and you keep all profits. To me, this is a much simpler way to run an FBA business.

Bonus #9 – Why Seasonal Products Sell Year Round on Amazon.com

Seasonal products are products that sell better during one season of the year than they do during other seasons. The easiest type of item to understand is Christmas items. They sell better at Christmas time. This should be no surprise, but it may surprise you to know that Christmas items sell all year long. Sure, they don't sell in the same quantity, but there is demand for Christmas items throughout the year. I don't always know why someone wants to buy Christmas items in July, but maybe they are having a Christmas-in-July party. The population is big enough that it would not surprise me to find out that some people simply celebrate Christmas during an entirely different time of year than December 25th.

Seasonal products also include items such as heaters and air conditioners. Not many retailers in Massachusetts are stocking and selling air conditioners in the wintertime or snow blowers in the spring. But while it may be cold in Massachusetts, it's warm in other parts of the country. I ran into this when I was looking to buy a small fan for a room that had a lot of computer equipment. The room got warm so I wanted a fan. Just try to find a store in Texas selling fans in the wintertime.

Even something as simple as differing climates can represent opportunities. As seasonal items get clearanced out in Texas, there is still a demand for those products in Massachusetts. Think about portable heaters. By the time it is warming up in Texas and all the heaters are on clearance, it's still snowing in Massachusetts. The supply and demand are not matched up due to the physical limitations of the real world. But through online sales channels, you are able to funnel this supply to the demand and keep the profit along the way.

Here is a story about a seasonal product that we purchased at retail and sold through FBA.

The product was an 8-foot long Thomas the Train holiday inflatable decoration. This product was a Home Depot exclusive item. This meant that you could either buy it from Home Depot or you could buy it on the secondary market from someone who bought it from Home Depot. Many people did not know that this was available at Home Depot and many people also did not live near a Home Depot. This was a destination type of item meaning that it was not entirely price-sensitive. People either want an 8-foot long Thomas the Train holiday inflatable decoration, or they don't. At a fair price, they will buy online. We bought these same items the previous year when we were still selling them as merchant fulfilled. This year, we anticipated good sales on the item so we had Home Depot order us 75 of them directly at $79 each. They gave us a bulk purchase discount and of course it was tax-free. We sent them all to FBA and they sold out prior to Christmas.

This was when we were traveling back and forth between Texas and Massachusetts. We were still in Massachusetts when my contact at Home Depot called and asked if I wanted to buy any more Thomas the Train decorations. It was after Christmas so at first I said no, but then I caught myself and asked how much. They had been marked down to $17! Sweet, but how many did they have? Just a few, right? Wrong. They had 81 of them sitting on their shelves. Why on earth did they have so many? Turns out, the Home Depot computer system had automatically ordered more, anticipating strong sales after I ordered 75 of them for our direct purchase. Of course there was no way that this store would ever sell that many. This spike in demand that my order put in the computer system was artificial demand, not real customer demand based on actual sales of the product to end users.

I told him that of course I wanted them all but that I was still in Massachusetts for another two months. He didn't care; he said as long as they were paid for, he would put them up in the overhead and I could pick them up in March. So that's what we did. I paid for them over the phone and picked them up in March. Now we were only in Texas for a few months before planning to come back to Massachusetts for the rest of the year. And now I had 81 holiday products sitting at my house. If I had the option, I would not have sent this seasonal, holiday item to FBA in April. But the FBA storage fees were so low that I decided it would be easiest to send them all to FBA now, even though it was nowhere near Christmas time. If I didn't, I wouldn't be back in time to send them in at all and I would miss Christmas altogether! Super bonus was that they were considered oversize and they went to the Texas oversize warehouse (all gone now) that was less than five miles from our house.

I fully expected them to sit in inventory all year while I paid FBA storage fees and waited on the surge of orders at Christmas time. I was surprised when month after month I sold some of these things. Some months I only sold one, and some months up to three, but every month I sold at least one. I did not expect this but it goes to show you that while demand may be reduced for seasonal items that are out of season, it does not go away completely. Someone, somewhere will still want them. Of course by Christmas time the rest of them sold out very quickly for a nice, handsome profit. Not the way I would have predicted the deal to have gone, but it was a profitable item to be sure.

Bonus #10 – Live vs. Local Database Scouting Services

So you're ready to start scouting for products to sell on Amazon. You've seen people with scanners, phones, and PDAs. You've seen the laser beams and heard the beeping. Which one is right for you? Are they all the same? What are the differences? I'm glad you asked!

ScanPower for iPhone and Android devices is what is called a LIVE scouting service. There are other types of scouting services that are called local database services. They were mentioned earlier in this book in Chapter 7 - The History of Scouting. They were the best option when wireless data connection speeds were simply not fast enough to support a live scouting service. With the widespread availability of Wi-Fi as well as 3G and 4G data networks, the advantages that the local database services enjoyed are becoming obsolete.

Live Data vs. Local Database – How They Work

Live scouting services send and retrieve pricing data as you request it. You scan a barcode, the program sends the request, and the pricing data is returned and displayed on your iPhone or Android device.

Local database services run on Windows Mobile PDAs and download a database of pricing data to a memory card. These services primarily cater to the book and media market. As an FBA seller, you need pricing data for much more than just books and media.

The advantages of having live data are simply unmatched. Pricing data is always available, always accurate, and always in sync with the latest market changes. Local database services will have old, stale data the moment that the data is done downloading. Prices and Sales Ranks change constantly.

The downside to using live data is that if you are in an area with no Wi-Fi, 3G or 4G service, your phone won't work and you'll be unable to retrieve pricing information. While these places do exist, they are becoming fewer and further between due to increased mobile broadband coverage and faster mobile broadband speed.

As mentioned in Chapter 7, when I carry my Sprint phone and my Verizon iPad (3rd generation), I can have access to Sprint, Verizon 4G, Verizon 3G, and even AT&T 3G with a SIM card. Finding a place with no service from any of these carriers would be difficult to do.

Limitations of a 2-Gigabyte (GB) Memory Card

There is a reason that local database services only use up to a maximum 2 GB memory card. This is because Windows Mobile PDAs (with a few, expensive exceptions) cannot read a memory card greater than 2 GB. A local database service will have a hard limit of how much pricing that they can provide of 2 GB. This means that they have to choose what pricing data to INCLUDE as well as what pricing data to EXCLUDE. When you sell using FBA, why would you want ANY pricing data excluded? What items are you going to exclude yourself from selling?

New Products Added to Amazon.com All the Time

Thousands of new products launch daily on Amazon.com. If a local database has not been updated in three days, then you have three days of new products that you would not even know exist! Some of the newest products are the hottest, most popular products that represent easy arbitrage opportunities.

Maintenance

ScanPower requires no maintenance. There is never anything to download or maintain. Local databases have to be constantly kept up to date.

Speed vs. Accuracy

One advantage that a local database service would enjoy over a live service would be speed. Since the pricing data is stored locally, the pricing data returns very quickly. With a live service, there can be several factors that will affect the time that it takes to return product information. Most items will return almost instantly, with speeds matching those of local databases. If your network speeds are slow, then data transfer can take longer. Pricing data can also take longer if an item has an abnormally high number of offers (most common when scanning books) as Scanpower has to sort hundreds, sometimes thousands of offers in order to correctly display the useful pricing information.

Speed is more important when you are scouting in highly competitive environments like day one of a library sale. In retail environments, things are much more relaxed.

ScanPower Exclusive Features

Being a live service allows ScanPower to do some pretty fancy things that are simply not possible with local database services.

Features like:

Displaying New, Used, Amazon, and FBA Offers for every item in every category on Amazon.com

FBA Net prices displayed (price + shipping)

Product image

Multiple item match search results

You can also always touch the product image displayed in ScanPower to go directly to the Amazon product page in your mobile browser. Complete and accurate data is always at your fingertips.

The importance of these features is discussed in more depth at the end of this book under Vendor Spotlight – ScanPower.

Summary

The advantages that ScanPower users enjoy in terms of complete, live, accurate data is simply unparalleled. It allows users to make the best buying decisions. Every item purchased for resale includes an inherent risk. Those risks are minimized when you have the best data. If you have anything less than the best data, then your risk for buying items that are not actually good for resale will increase. The best data also helps you to not pass over opportunities that you would miss if you were using inferior data.

The number of places that have no Wi-Fi service and absolutely no data service from any cellular provider do exist, but they are few and far between. They dwarf in comparison to 'everywhere else' where there are ample arbitrage opportunities. The last useful feature of the local database, working without a data connection, is slowly becoming irrelevant.

Ultimate Scouting Weapon: Verizon LTE iPad

The Verizon LTE iPad is my choice for the ultimate scouting weapon. You can get an iPad with an inexpensive data plan ($20/month) with no contract. Just pay for the months that you need it. The Verizon LTE iPad has awesome 4G LTE coverage as well as Verizon 3G coverage. You can even put in an AT&T SIM card and use AT&T 3G service if you find a place with absolutely no Verizon coverage. You can also use the iPad as a hotspot for no extra charge and share the data with other devices.

The screen is big and easy to read. Use it as a GPS and plan your scouting route. The battery life is also awesome.

Additional Resources

Did you know that you could get an Amazon FBA Specialist to walk you through your first FBA shipment right over the phone? Getting started with FBA couldn't be easier! Here's how:

http://www.amazonservices.com/content/sellers-contact-amazon.htm/

Fill out the form and choose that you are interested in Fulfillment by Amazon, already sell on Amazon, and want help with starting FBA. It will go straight to the FBA Launch Specialist Team.

https://sellercentral.amazon.com/gp/fbacalc/fba-calculator.html
This is the official Amazon FBA Calculator that you can use to evaluate FBA fees and determine an item's profitability

ScanPower.com
Information about the ScanPower family of services, educational information, videos, podcasts, discussion, and more.

facebook.com/groups/scanpower
ScanPower Facebook Discussion Group – Facebook group discussing Amazon, FBA, arbitrage (online & retail), as well as ScanPower news and updates.

facebook.com/scanpower
ScanPower Facebook Fan Page – exclusive links, tips, and strategies are shared here. 'Like' us to get all of the latest updates.

ScanPower on SpreeCast – spreecast.com/users/chrisgreen
SpreeCast channel for LIVE scouting events, video demonstrations, and radio commentary.

ScanPower TV - YouTube.com/ScanPowerTV
YouTube channel of ScanPower videos including account setup and support videos.

Thrifting-with-the-boys.com
Educational (and fun!) website focused on sourcing products for resale from thrift stores. They have a Facebook Group as well.

http://www.amazonsellersupportblog.com/
Amazon Seller Support Blog

Terapeak.com
EBay research tools and eBay market data that go back further than just viewing 'completed items' on eBay.

WorthPoint.com
The largest resource for researching and valuing your art, antiques & collectibles.

RankTracer.com
This site will track an item's Sales Rank on Amazon for a monthly fee. This is the site we used to make the graphs seen in Chapter 13.

BookSaleFinder.com
BookSaleFinder is a great FREE site to find book and library sales in your area.

I am a firm believer in the power of an idea. One idea can be turned into something big. A $20 book only needs to give you one idea that you can use to make more than $20 for that book to be considered worthwhile. The right idea or the right information can be the difference between a good year and a great year.

An example of this is when I first learned that you could buy a UPC and create your own product pages on Amazon. I had been emailing Amazon customer support about how to do this and they wrote back that the only way that they knew of was to purchase a UPC. Until then, I did not know that you could even purchase a UPC. This one little piece of information has been incredibly valuable to me. It's hard to put a price tag on information, but always remember to continue to learn and try new things. If not, you run the risk of running a stale business model, which is incredibly risky in today's (increasingly) ever-changing marketplace.

Recommended Reading

These books will change the way you see Amazon, FBA, eBay, and selling online. They are invaluable to learning how to sell smart and not just work hard. Learning the WHY behind why things work the way that they do is pivotal to long-term success.

Book #1 – The Long Tail

By Chris Anderson

amazon.com/gp/product/1401309666

This book will open your mind about how Amazon is able to profit by selling fewer quantities of a larger selection of products. FBA + The Long Tail is a powerful combination.

There is more money to be made in the tail, than in the bestsellers. Amazon figured this out years ago and the rest is history.

Book #2 – How to Sell at Margins Higher Than Your Competitors

By Lawrence L. Steinmetz & William T. Brooks

amazon.com/gp/product/0471744832

This book will blow your mind in terms of pricing and how to price your items. It will also show you that competing only on price is simply not necessary. **Remember, this is a margins game, not a volume game.** This book will prove it to you.